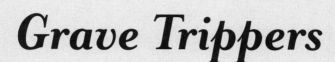

Grave Trippers

HISTORY AT OUR FEET

Robert and Vincent Gardino

Camino Books, Inc.
PHILADELPHIA

Manufactured in the United States of America
1 2 3 4   22 21 20 19

Library of Congress Cataloging-in-Publication Data

Names: Gardino, Robert, 1957– author. | Gardino, Vincent, 1953– author.
Title: Grave trippers : history at our feet / by Robert Gardino and Vincent Gardino.
Description: Philadelphia : Camino Books, Inc., [2019]
Identifiers: LCCN 2019030735 (print) | LCCN 2019030736 (ebook) |
    ISBN 9781680980363 (paperback) | ISBN 9781680980370 (ebook)
Subjects: LCSH: Cemeteries—United States—Guidebooks. | Celebrities—United
    States—Biography. | Celebrities—Tombs—United States—Guidebooks. | Historic
    sites—United States—Guidebooks.
Classification: LCC E159 .G218 2019 (print) | LCC E159 (ebook) |
    DDC 363.7/50973—dc23
LC record available at https://lccn.loc.gov/2019030735
LC ebook record available at https://lccn.loc.gov/2019030736

ISBN 978-1-68098-036-3

ISBN 978-1-68098-037-0 (ebook)

Interior design: P. M. Gordon Associates, Inc.
Cover design: Jerilyn DiCarlo

This book is available at a special discount on bulk purchases for educational, business, and promotional purposes. For information write:

Publisher
Camino Books, Inc.
P.O. Box 59026
Philadelphia, PA 19102
www.caminobooks.com

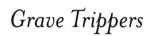

Grave Trippers

*This book is dedicated to the following,
without whose influence this labor of love
would not have been possible:*

*With love, affection, and respect
to our parents, Nino and Lina,
and also to
Jinny, Beloved Wife and Sister-in-Law.
We miss them every day.*

Contents

Foreword

JAMES McPHERSON

Over a period of about a dozen years, my wife Pat and I toured most of the principal Civil War battlefields with the Gardino brothers and their friends Bob and Patrice Martin. As keen students of the American Civil War, we shared the conviction that the best way to learn about and understand those battles was to walk the ground and experience the terrain where they took place. This understanding concerned more than tactics and command decisions, though these things were important. Even more significant was the profound sense of empathy with the men who fought there, why they fought and how their experiences fit into the larger story of the war and its meaning in history. To walk these hallowed grounds connected us with the past through the "mystic chords of memory" that Abraham Lincoln invoked in his first inaugural address.

These emotions were reinforced by our walks through the soldiers' cemeteries that are part of most Civil War battlefield parks. A poignant awareness of the sacrifice made by soldiers who gave, in Lincoln's phrase, "the last full measure of devotion" to the cause for which they fought was overwhelming. Cemeteries provide an even more powerful sense of the connection between the present and the past, the living and the dead, than do battlefields, buildings, or any other part of the environment. This is true not only for soldiers who died in war but also for people in all walks of life—and death. The mortal remains of those who have gone before us help us to comprehend how the world we live in came to be.

In this unique and fascinating book, Vincent and Robert Gardino tell the stories of 70 Americans buried in more than a dozen cemeteries, churches, and tombs in the United States. The lives of these men and women span almost three centuries of American history. Most of them were prominent, some famous; a few were humble and obscure, but their graves evoke uncommon points of interest. They include actors, writers, musicians, athletes, military heroes, politicians, and ten presidents of the United States plus Confederate President Jefferson Davis. The mini-biographies of these people offer important information and sometimes amusing sidelights on their careers. Collectively these biographies constitute a rich tapestry of American history. Many of the graves are adorned by elaborate tombstones or statuary that the Gardinos have photographed for inclusion as illustrations in this book. The authors have also provided precise directions to guide readers who wish to visit the graves themselves.

And if you become a grave tripper in the footsteps of the Gardino brothers, you may soon find your own way to many other graves in these and other cemeteries whose inhabitants' stories can enrich your awareness of those mystic chords of memory that connect the living to the dead. So, *Bon Voyage* for your trip into the past marked by stones of granite and marble.

Grave Trippers

Introduction

"You have got to be kidding!" I cried out in tired exasperation. (This is Robert speaking.) My brother Vincent had just informed me that we were in the wrong section of Mount Auburn Cemetery in our quest to locate the final resting place of Edwin Booth, brother of famed Lincoln assassin John Wilkes Booth.

We had already spent a good portion of the day trying to locate another famous individual's grave, that of Henry Wadsworth Longfellow, the great American poet. Longfellow is probably most remembered for the poem popularly known as "The Midnight Ride of Paul Revere." It took climbing up a relatively steep hill, but we were successful in finding the Longfellow gravesite. But finding Booth's grave was turning out to be more problematic.

"So where should we be?" I asked Vincent as we looked intently at the cemetery's map, provided free of charge at Mount Auburn Cemetery's front office. Vincent informed me that we were in section seven of the cemetery, but Edwin Booth's grave was in section six, which we had overshot. Weary from walking most of the day, I gave Vincent a quick angry glare. But Vincent, still studying the map, said, "We have to backtrack a little, to Mound Avenue, then we have to keep our eyes peeled for a smaller road called Pyrola Path, which should get us to Booth." "We hope!" I shot back. Vincent said, "Sorry, Robert," but I told him to forget it as I'd been guilty of the same sin countless times in the past at different cemeteries. As it turned out, we weren't as far away from the grave as we had thought.

Not long after we found Pyrola Path, our dispositions changed

1

sharply when one of us spotted something a short distance away. "There he is! He is right over there. See it?" And within a minute we stood in front of Edwin Booth's impressive burial site.

Our grave tripping that day at Mount Auburn Cemetery was successful. We had found both Longfellow's and Booth's resting places. Our hobby of visiting the graves/tombs/crypts of famous people or notables had brought us a high level of satisfaction.

It was during the long Memorial Day weekend of 1995 that we made our first joint visit to Washington, DC. Only one of us had been there previously, and those past trips were work-related, affording scant time to visit the city's famous landmarks. In planning our trip we had put together a tentative itinerary of what we wanted to see. We had agreed we would try to see many of "the usual suspects" in DC tourist sites, such as the Capitol Building, the Lincoln Memorial, the Smithsonian, and the Supreme Court. Also included in our itinerary was Arlington National Cemetery, where we hoped to see President John F. Kennedy's grave. Though we were very young at the time, we both had distinct memories of the Kennedy assassination. We remembered watching on television the procession of the horse-driven caisson with Kennedy's flag-draped casket as it went on to Arlington. We were transfixed, our eyes glued to a black-and-white TV set. It was a majestic spectacle despite being a sad event. The last thing we remember of that telecast was the haunting image of Jackie Kennedy lighting the eternal flame at her husband's grave.

Washington, DC, as you would expect, is rich in the details of the workings of American government and its history. On that first visit in 1995, we thoroughly enjoyed virtually everything we saw. But our trip to Arlington National Cemetery was our number one highlight. The grounds of Arlington are pristine and exceptionally well maintained. The solemn and dignified rows of predominately short white headstones, marking the graves of men and women who served in America's military, is an impressive sight. Also striking are the tombs of the unknown soldiers and the remarkable visual of the changing of the guard. JFK's gravesite, which includes the final resting place of his wife, Jackie Kennedy Onassis, is befitting a president of the United States. The grave's design is simple yet grand.

Our visit to Kennedy's grave reignited our interest in reading more about John Kennedy's life and presidency. In addition, after seeing Kennedy's grave we visited the grave of the only other president buried in Arlington, William Howard Taft. He is the only president who went on to become chief justice of the Supreme Court. His relationship with Theodore Roosevelt had eerie parallels to the relationship of John Adams and Thomas Jefferson. Both these sets of presidents started off as the best of friends, then their relationships became strained to the point that neither spoke to the other for years, though in the end there was at least a partial reconciliation.

We were staggered to discover the many other famous individuals who were veterans and entitled to be buried at Arlington—people such as heavyweight boxing champion Joe Louis and Academy Award–winning actor Lee Marvin, who will both be highlighted in this book. When we got home from our trip, we both researched what other famous individuals' graves were located near where we lived. And though we couldn't have known at the time, *Grave Trippers* was born right then and there.

We have often been asked why we have this fascination with visiting cemeteries and the graves of historical figures. We do not consider ourselves morbid individuals, and we are not obsessed with the subject of death. Cemeteries are usually of no appeal to us unless they contain graves of individuals of historic or notable significance. We are not into paranormal activity, and we are not trying to communicate with anyone from the great beyond. We admire many in history, as well as those in the entertainment and sports fields. By visiting the final resting places of those who spark our interest, we have the opportunity to connect with them in a certain way. As much as we would be thrilled to be in the living presence of, say, George Washington, that obviously cannot be done. Visiting where his remains lie in Mount Vernon is the closest we can come to actually being with him. It is also a gesture of respect we wish conveyed to the deceased.

We were both born and have lived our entire lives in New York City. We grew up on the west side of Manhattan, in an area still affectionately referred to as Hell's Kitchen, very close to Times Square, the celebrated heart of the Broadway Theater District. Our beginnings were humble, but we had parents who instilled in us the value of a good education. We were always encouraged to read and broaden our interests. Our father, in our younger years, worked as a waiter in a celebrity hangout restaurant by the name of Danny's Hideaway. We can still remember the thrill we would get when our father occasionally brought home celebrity autographs. The autographs, which were inscribed to the two of us, were often signed in pencil on short white pieces of paper from our father's order pad. Two of the nicest autographs our father brought home were from legendary television variety show host Ed Sullivan and screen legend Robert Mitchum. We still have them and they now hang framed on one of our home walls.

As we got a little older, our love for those autographs our father brought home remained, and we were determined to add to the small collection. As young boys growing up in the 1960s, we did not have a lot of money, so purchasing them was out of the question. We had discovered in one of New York's midtown libraries a series of volumes titled *Who's Who in America*, which provided addresses for celebrities, politicians, sports figures, and other notable personalities. Heaven knows the exact number of requests for autographs we mailed out using addresses from *Who's Who*. Suffice it to say that it was a lot! Those early letters were all handwritten, usually on writing-pad pages with the typical straight horizontal blue rows. The requests were basically straightforward, usually stating how old we were and that we had an autograph collection to which we'd love to add this person's autograph. On the weekends we would, between the two of us, prepare

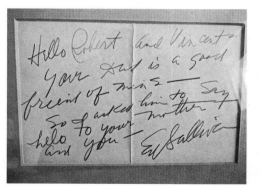 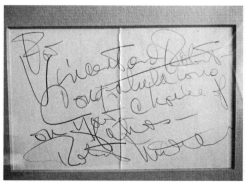

Autographs of Ed Sullivan (left) and Robert Mitchum

on average 10 to 15 letters that were mailed out promptly on Monday morning. We learned at an early age the value of bulk: by mailing out numerous autograph requests at a time, we were bound to receive at least a few responses that made our efforts worthwhile. In fact, to our delight, the vast majority of requests were answered. The largest percentage of responses came from politicians. Our correspondence from politicians included handsome letters from former President Harry Truman, then Governor of California Ronald Reagan, former Vice President Hubert Humphrey, and then Massachusetts Senator Edward Kennedy.

Vincent did something that I think was positively brilliant in the way he obtained then President Richard Nixon's autograph. The president of the United States, no matter who he or she may be, receives so much mail from the general populace that the odds of getting a response are close to zero. Vincent, like Grant at Vicksburg, took a circuitous route. Vincent wrote to then First Lady Pat Nixon and asked her to please obtain her husband's autograph for him. A few weeks later, he received an envelope from the office of the First Lady. The envelope contained a brief note from Mrs. Nixon, and on a small White House card was President Nixon's signature. Kudos to Vincent and, for her kindness, a special thank-you to the memory and spirit of Pat Nixon.

Point of note: each of us has a complete set of all the presidents' signatures from Washington to Trump.

As time progressed we expanded our requests to include appropriate questions for the individual we were writing to. Most of our questions centered on that individual's career. Occasionally we would ask for general advice: for instance, if we wanted to enter their field of occupation, what would they suggest? Politicians in general love these questions, and they often added more information than was asked for. A case in point was a response we received from Burton Kendall Wheeler. A Democratic senator from Montana, Wheeler was the vice presidential running mate of Wisconsin Republican Senator Robert La Follette when La Follette ran for president in 1924 on the Progressive Party ticket. (Calvin Coolidge was elected in a landslide that year.) We asked Mr. Wheeler whether he thought he and La Follette could have won the election had they "more money" to run their campaign.

Wheeler responded that it was difficult to speculate, but he remembered that La Follette actually thought they had a chance to win. In addition, Wheeler provided us with a juicy tidbit about Joseph P. Kennedy, future ambassador to Great Britain and father of John, Robert, and Edward Kennedy. Joseph P. Kennedy had told Wheeler directly that he was spreading disinformation to labor unions and their members, saying La Follette was not a friend to labor and advocated policies that would lead to the destruction of unions.

It was responses such as Wheeler's that fueled our interest in history. We wanted to read and learn more about individuals and events that piqued our curiosity. Our avid interest in history and autographs continues to this day, and we think it has led us to the avocation of grave tripping, another opportunity to come into indirect contact with history makers.

We hope you enjoy this volume about many of our favorite cemeteries and the graves of famous individuals contained therein. In covering the men and women in this volume, we have done our best to provide accurate directions to the graves. As veteran Grave Trippers, we know very well the frustration of trying to find a particular site. The maps provided by cemeteries, if there are any, can be frustratingly difficult to understand. Some of those maps can be just plain wrong. Directions provided by individuals who work at a cemetery's front office can also sometimes be maddening. Road signs within cemeteries may be seemingly impossible to find. Even when you are in the right area of a cemetery, you may need a lot of patience and some luck to find a particular grave.

For each cemetery we discuss, the individuals we cover represent not an exhaustive list but simply our favorites. We did our best to choose a cross section of men and women in a variety of professions. The names of some are well known, while many we feel are not remembered as well as they should be. In each profile we try to convey why each individual has special meaning to us.

We had a lot of fun putting this all together. We think you will find what follows informative and different. For each historical individual we cover, there will be some history of that person and, when possible, some fun facts you may not have known. When you are finished with this book, we hope you too will be ignited with a renewed enthusiasm for the history of people who have impacted our lives.

So let's get started. The fun is on us. Perhaps eventually you will consider yourself a Grave Tripper too!

CHAPTER ONE

Arlington National Cemetery

ARLINGTON, VIRGINIA 22211

This grand, impressive, and dignified cemetery was established during the American Civil War for the burial of fallen Union soldiers. Comprised of 624 acres, the vast property is owned by the United States Department of the Army. Approximately 400,000 veterans spanning numerous American conflicts from the Civil War to the present, as well as many veterans' family members, are interred there.

The Arlington property was originally purchased in 1802 by George Washington Parke Custis. George was the grandson of Martha Washington, and his daughter Mary Anna in 1831 married Robert E. Lee, the future famed Confederate army general. Custis constructed his home on this property. That residence, which still exists today on the cemetery grounds, is known as the Arlington House.

Four years after Mary Anna inherited the property from her father, the state of Virginia seceded from the Union, and Mary Anna's husband resigned from the Union Army to command the Confederate force of the Army of Northern Virginia. As her property was just over the Potomac River from Washington, DC, Mary Anna knew that the Union Army would seize it. She abandoned her home, and the Union did take the property shortly afterward. After the Wilderness Campaign in 1864, which pitted Ulysses S. Grant against Robert E. Lee for the first time, fallen Army soldiers were buried on the grounds of Arlington.

This cemetery is open every day of the year, and tours are readily available for a fee. Hours, depending on the season, are from 8 a.m. to 7 p.m. or 8 a.m. to 5 p.m.

JOHN F. KENNEDY
U.S. President
Born: May 29, 1917
Died: November 22, 1963

As we indicated in the Introduction, it was the haunting memory of watching JFK's funeral on television years before that prompted us to visit the grave of the 35th president of the United States.

Kennedy was born in Massachusetts to Joseph P. and Rose Kennedy. He graduated from Harvard in 1940, then joined the U.S. Navy during World War II. During the war he commanded a series of PT boats. Kennedy was awarded the Navy and Marine Corps medal for heroism for saving the life of a badly burned crewmember on one of his patrol boats, the *PT-109*, which was rammed by a Japanese destroyer and cut in half.

Following the war, Kennedy was elected to the House of Representatives in 1946 and subsequently reelected in 1948 and 1950. In 1952 he ran for the U.S. Senate, defeating popular incumbent Henry Cabot Lodge in an upset. He won the Pulitzer Prize in 1957 for his book *Profiles in Courage*. In 1958 he was reelected to the Senate in a landslide victory. In 1960 he decided to seek the office of president of the United States. He won the Democratic Party nomination, defeating a crowded field. In November of that year he defeated the Republican nominee, Vice President Richard M. Nixon, in an extremely close election.

President Kennedy was killed by an assassin's bullet in Dallas, Texas, on November 22, 1963. Despite a 1964 presidential commission's conclusion that JFK was killed by a lone gunman, Lee Harvey Oswald, conspiracy theories continue to abound.

FUN FACT

John F. Kennedy, at age 43, was the youngest man ever elected president. However, he is not the youngest man ever sworn in as president. That honor belongs to Theodore Roosevelt. In 1901 Roosevelt was 42 when, as vice president, he assumed the office upon the death of President William McKinley.

John F. Kennedy's Grave

DIRECTIONS

You will need to obtain a cemetery map from the Visitors Center. Immediately behind section 5 on the map, you will see the memorial area that houses the grave of John Kennedy. It is clearly visible by the white steps leading to this section.

JACQUELINE KENNEDY ONASSIS

U.S. First Lady
Born: July 28, 1929
Died: May 19, 1994

It is not possible to remember John Kennedy's funeral and not recall the strong and dignified presence of his widow at that event. Despite her grief Jackie Kennedy demonstrated to the world a grace that contributed to her being much admired and popular until her own death.

Jacqueline Kennedy Onassis was born on Long Island to John and Janet Bouvier. Raised in an affluent environment, she became a highly skilled horseback rider, winning several equestrian competitions in her youth. In college she studied French literature, graduating from George Washington University in 1951. Following graduation, she landed a job as the "Inquiring Camera Girl" for the *Washington Times-Herald* newspaper. Ironically, in 1953 she interviewed then Vice President Richard Nixon, who would go on to run against her husband in the 1960 election.

In May 1952 she met then Massachusetts Congressman John F. Kennedy. They were married the following year in September. The marriage produced daughter Caroline in 1957 and son John in 1960. Two other children did not survive: Arabella was stillborn in 1956, and Patrick died shortly after a premature birth in 1963; both are interred at Arlington with their parents.

During the presidential campaign of 1960 Jackie proved to be a strong asset for her husband. She worked tirelessly, granting interviews, filming commercials, and writing a syndicated newspaper column.

As First Lady she dedicated much of her time to transforming the White House to make it not only the first family's residence, but also a celebration of the country's historic past and culture. She accomplished this by obtaining past presidents' furniture, art, and artifacts. Also, as First Lady she began the tradition of recognizing and inviting the country's great musical artists to the White House to perform.

Five years after JFK was assassinated, Jacqueline Kennedy married Greek shipping tycoon Aristotle Onassis. They remained married until his death in 1975. She later became an editor at Viking Press, and eventually a senior editor at Doubleday. After a relatively short bout with lymphoma she passed away in her Fifth Avenue apartment in New York in 1994. In a second irony involving Richard Nixon, Jackie Kennedy died just slightly less than one month after Nixon.

FUN FACT

Jackie Kennedy won an honorary Emmy for her work in a CBS television special, for which she conducted a tour of the newly restored White House. It was estimated that more than 50 million Americans watched the special the night it aired.

DIRECTIONS

Same as for John F. Kennedy.

Jackie Kennedy's Grave

JOE LOUIS
Heavyweight Boxing Champion
Born: May 13, 1914
Died: April 12, 1981

Our father was a huge boxing fan, and he would describe to us the excitement of just hearing on the radio Joe Louis's many title-defending bouts. We too became boxing fans, especially of Joe Louis's career.

A native son of Alabama, Joe Louis Barrow was born into a poor family. As a child Joe was often perceived as unintelligent because he had limited schooling and spoke with a stammer. He took boxing lessons as a teenager and turned professional in 1934. Soon after, he became known as the "Brown Bomber" due to his punching ability.

In June 1937 Louis knocked out James J. Braddock in the eighth round to become the heavyweight champion of the world. Exactly one year later he avenged his only previous professional loss, demolishing Max Schmeling in just over two minutes of the first round. Louis held the heavyweight boxing crown an unprecedented 11 years and 8 months. In that period he defended the title a record 26 times.

After retiring from boxing, Louis was plagued by financial problems because of unpaid taxes owed the IRS. It wasn't until years later

Joe Louis's Grave

that the IRS forgave Louis's tax bill as the result of his third wife's appeals as his attorney. Joe spent much of his later years as a greeter at Caesar's Palace casino in Las Vegas. He died in 1981 after a massive heart attack.

FUN FACT

In 1993 Joe Louis became the first boxer to have his likeness appear on a U.S. postage stamp.

DIRECTIONS

Take Memorial Avenue to Schley Drive. Turn left on Schley Drive. Turn right on Roosevelt Drive. In Section 7A turn right to stay on grave row. Louis is about 25 feet into Section 7A with his large and impressive monument.

LEE MARVIN

Academy Award–Winning Actor
Born: February 19, 1924
Died: August 29, 1987

Lee Marvin was such a talented actor that when he played the role of a mean and nasty heavy in a movie, it was difficult not to be drawn in rather than repelled by the character.

Lee Marvin was born in New York City, and as a young boy he proved to be incorrigible, often getting into trouble for bad behavior. In 1942, at the age of 18, he enlisted in the Marine Corps Reserve and served in the South Pacific during World War II. In 1944 he was hit by enemy gunfire, and as a result had his sciatic nerve severed. In the same battle he was shot in the foot. For his wounds he was awarded a purple heart.

After the war his acting career started by chance when he was asked to stand in for a theater actor who had fallen ill. Being a recent marine veteran served him well, as many of his early roles were in war pictures. Besides acting in those roles, he advised directors about how to make war scenes as realistic as possible.

As the result of his persona and distinctive voice, he was often cast as a "bad guy" in movies such as *The Wild One* with Marlin Brando,

Bad Day at Black Rock with Spencer Tracy, and *The Man Who Shot Liberty Valance* with John Wayne. Ironically, he won the Oscar in 1966 for playing twins in the comedy *Cat Ballou*.

In 1979 he was sued by his longtime live-in girlfriend, Michelle Triola. She sued on the basis that, after their breakup, she was entitled to compensation and support under the laws of California regarding alimony and community property. As a result of this case, the term *palimony* was introduced into the legal lexicon. Triola was initially awarded $104,000, but on appeal a higher court reversed her award, noting that there was no evidence of any written or verbal contract between the two parties entitling her to shared community property.

FUN FACTS

1. Lee Marvin was a descendant of Confederate General Robert E. Lee and was named after him.
2. Marvin's grave in Arlington is side by side with that of boxing champion Joe Louis.

DIRECTIONS

Same as for Joe Louis.

Lee Marvin's Grave

WILLIAM HOWARD TAFT
U.S. President
Born: September 15, 1857
Died: March 8, 1930

What fascinates us about Taft is that, unlike the vast majority of those who run for the office of president, Taft would have honestly preferred not to be a candidate. But a particular friendship compelled him to seek the office.

Taft came from a prominent Ohio family. He was easygoing by nature, and his successes in school and early professional career were attributed mostly to his hard work rather than to a keen intellect. Taft developed a reputation for honesty and was considered fair-minded.

In 1880 Taft earned his law degree from Cincinnati Law School. At the young age of 29 he was appointed a judge on the Superior Court of Cincinnati. In 1889, at age 32, he was considered by President Benjamin Harrison for the Supreme Court, but was chosen instead to be U.S. solicitor general. In 1900 President William McKinley appointed Taft to head a commission to help lead the Philippine Islands to self-rule. Taft lived in the Philippines for four years as its civilian governor. In 1904 he returned to the United States to become President Theodore Roosevelt's secretary of war.

Theodore Roosevelt and William Howard Taft had been close personal friends since they met in 1890. Taft would have preferred being appointed chief justice of the Supreme Court, but both Roosevelt and Taft's wife Nellie pushed him to run for president in 1908. In November of that year Taft won a comfortable victory. During Taft's administration, however, Roosevelt had a series of policy disagreements with him, and their friendship became strained. In 1912 Roosevelt ran for president as the "Bull Moose" Progressive Party nominee. Taft and Roosevelt split the Republican vote that November, allowing Woodrow Wilson to win the presidency. Shortly before Roosevelt passed away in January 1919, he and Taft reconciled after meeting by chance in a Washington hotel dining room. At Roosevelt's funeral Taft was observed crying.

After leaving the White House, Taft became a law professor at Yale. In 1921 President Warren Harding finally appointed Taft to his

William Howard Taft's Grave

long–desired position as chief justice of the Supreme Court, where he would serve until one month before his death in 1930.

FUN FACTS

1. Taft is the only man to have served as both president and chief justice.
2. Not only are William Howard Taft and John F. Kennedy the only presidents currently buried at Arlington, but one of Kennedy's chapters in his Pulitzer Prize–winning book *Profiles in Courage* is on Senator Robert Taft, President Taft's son.

DIRECTIONS

Take Memorial Avenue to Schley Drive. Turn right on Schley Drive. This will be Section 30. Taft is approximately 75 feet down Schley Drive. You will see a path that leads about 50 feet to his memorial space, which includes a bench.

ILONA MASSEY

Film Actress/Singer
Born: June 16, 1910
Died: August 20, 1974

We suspect that many readers are asking themselves, "Who?" Those who do recognize her name may be asking, "She's at Arlington?" That latter question we pondered ourselves when we discovered her final resting place. No, she wasn't ever a part of the American military, but her spouse Donald Dawson was. Dawson was a major general in the

Ilona Massey's Grave

Air Force Reserve. Interestingly, Dawson was a political advisor to President Harry S. Truman and was instrumental in putting together Truman's 1948 presidential election whistle-stop campaign.

Ilona Massey was a Hungarian-born thespian. Her distinctive voice and sultry good looks got her billed as "the next Dietrich." Her body of work included not only movies but also stage, television, and radio stints. However, if it weren't for one movie in particular, it is doubtful she would be remembered. That movie was the B classic Universal horror film *Frankenstein Meets the Wolf Man* from 1943. She played Dr. Frankenstein's daughter Elsa. In that movie she is the only one, curiously, who has a heavy accent. The title "monsters" in that film were played by Lon Chaney, Jr., as the Wolf Man and an aging Bela Lugosi as Frankenstein's Monster.

Massey died in 1974 as the result of complications from cancer.

FUN FACT

In *Frankenstein Meets the Wolf Man"* Ilona Massey received top billing over both Lon Chaney, Jr., and Bela Lugosi.

DIRECTIONS

From Memorial Avenue proceed in a straight line through section 31. When you reach section 5, the grave of Ilona Massey will be in the front row. The name of her husband Donald Dawson is visible from the path; Ilona's name is on the back of the marker.

ROBERT LINCOLN

Secretary of War/Son of Abraham Lincoln
Born: August 1, 1843
Died: July 26, 1926

Born in Illinois, Robert was the first of four sons of Abraham and Mary Todd Lincoln. He was the only one of the four to live a long life, as his three brothers all died at very young ages. Shortly before the end of the Civil War, Robert enlisted in the Union Army and was assigned to General Ulysses Grant's administrative staff at the rank of captain. Robert was present at Appomattox when Confederate General Robert E. Lee surrendered to Grant.

Robert Lincoln's Grave

Following his father's assassination, he completed his legal studies at the University of Chicago and began to practice corporate law. In 1877 he declined to join President Rutherford B. Hayes's cabinet as secretary of state, but four years later accepted the position of secretary of war in James Garfield's cabinet. In 1889 President Benjamin Harrison appointed him to be minister to Great Britain.

After his government service Robert was general counsel to the Pullman Car Company, which manufactured locomotive cars. He later became chairman of the board of Pullman, retiring in 1922.

Robert Lincoln died of a cerebral hemorrhage in 1926. He is the only one of Abraham Lincoln's sons not interred near his father in Springfield, Illinois.

FUN FACTS

1. Robert Lincoln was in Washington, DC, when his father was killed. Amazingly, he was also in Washington when President James Garfield was shot, and he was in Buffalo, New York, when

President William McKinley was gunned down. This fact was not lost on Robert. After declining a presidential invitation, he stated, "No, I am not going and they'd better not ask me because there is a certain fatality about Presidential functions when I am present."

2. President Lincoln's first inaugural address, which contained the immortal phrase "by the better angels of our nature," was almost lost by Robert as he misplaced it when he and his father were traveling to Washington. Luckily it was located.

DIRECTIONS

At Memorial Avenue turn right on Schley Drive. Go to the corner of Section 31. Make left at the pathway at the corner of Section 31. Proceed halfway down that path in Section 31 and you will see Robert Lincoln's huge rectangular gravestone.

ROBERT PEARY

First Explorer to Reach North Pole (Maybe)
Born: May 6, 1856
Died: February 20, 1920

On a recent trip to Arlington, we were disappointed when no one got off the tour bus with us at the grave of Robert Peary. Peary was an American of great accomplishment, and we hope that by including him in this volume we can ignite further interest in his contributions to the field of exploration.

Robert Peary was born in Pennsylvania but spent most of his younger years in Maine. He was an excellent student, and after graduating from college he started out as a civil engineer. But small-town life in New England did not provide Peary with enough excitement, and in 1881 he enlisted in the Navy's civil engineer corps.

In 1887 Peary met African American Matthew Henson and discovered two commonalities: like Perry, Henson had experience at sea and was enthusiastic about exploring. Henson would accompany Peary on all of Peary's Arctic expeditions.

Peary's goal was to reach the North Pole. His first attempt came during his 1893–1894 expedition through Greenland. Because of a

Robert Peary's Grave

shortage of food, the final goal was not achieved. A second attempt to reach the North Pole, in 1905, was doomed by bad weather. On April 6, 1909, on his third expedition, Peary reached the North Pole—or so he announced. Many today dispute this claim, calculating that Peary was anywhere from 30 to 60 miles short of the pole.

The extremely harsh Arctic weather Peary experienced in his numerous expeditions caused him to age prematurely, and he died at age 63 in 1920.

DIRECTIONS

At Memorial Avenue take a right onto Eisenhower Drive, and follow that to the end, where you will hit Patton Drive. Turn right and go past Section 8A until you reach Section 8. Walk about 150 feet past the large part of Section 8, and you will see that it narrows. Turn right and walk across this narrow patch up a slight incline until you reach Jessup Drive and see the Coast Guard monument. Peary's impressive gravesite with a globe is clearly visible.

MATTHEW HENSON
Explorer
Born: August 8, 1866
Died: March 9, 1955

Like Peary, Matthew Henson is not remembered as we feel he should be. Born in Maryland, Henson was the son of two free-born African American sharecroppers. At a very young age he was employed as a cabin boy, and in the subsequent years he garnered seamanship experience traveling to Europe, Asia, and Africa.

A long-term working relationship was established in 1887 when Henson met Robert Peary. Matthew would accompany Peary on all

Matthew Henson's Grave

his Arctic expeditions, and he was with Peary when Peary claimed to have reached the North Pole in 1909. Matthew Henson was Peary's right-hand man, serving as navigator and craftsman. In addition, Henson learned the Inuit language and was able to serve as Peary's interpreter when necessary.

In 1912 Henson had his memoirs published under the title *A Negro Explorer at the North Pole*. In 1937 he was the first African American to be asked to join the highly regarded Explorers Club in New York City. At the age of 88 in 1955, Matthew Henson passed away and was buried at Woodlawn Cemetery in the Bronx.

FUN FACT

Under a presidential order issued by Ronald Reagan in 1988, Henson and his wife's remains were exhumed and reinterred in Arlington National Cemetery. Today Henson's plot is directly across from Robert Peary's final resting place.

DIRECTIONS

Same as for Robert Peary. Henson's grave is directly across from Peary's.

DANIEL E. SICKLES
Union General/Politician
Born: October 20, 1819
Died: May 3, 1914

Despite a dubious reputation, Dan Sickles, a first-class American historical rogue, will always have a soft spot in our hearts. That is because we were involved in having his gravestone upgraded. Let us explain. Our interest in Sickles began during a Gettysburg battlefield tour when our good friend and acclaimed Civil War historian James McPherson informed us of Sickles's peculiar role in that infamous battle. Further research into Sickles led us to visit his grave at Arlington. We were surprised to see that his weathered gravestone did not have the gold-leaf lettering generally accorded to veterans awarded the Congressional Medal of Honor and buried at Arlington. Upon our return to New York, we contacted the superintendent of Arlington to ask about the absence of gold leaf on Sickles's stone. Initially doubtful that Sickles

Daniel Sickles's Grave

was a congressional medal recipient, the superintendent looked into the matter. After several more follow-ups and two subsequent visits to Arlington, we beheld Sickles' new stone with gold lettering!

To call Daniel Sickles a colorful character would be an understatement. He was born in New York City to an affluent family. He studied at NYU and was admitted to the bar in 1846. In 1847 Sickles began his political career with his election to the New York State Assembly.

In 1852 he married Teresa Bagioli. Both families were opposed to the marriage. He was 33, she only 15 or 16. Neither one proved faithful to their marriage vows. Sickles was soon censured by the New York State Assembly for bringing a prostitute into the Assembly's chambers.

In 1859 Sickles discovered that his wife was having an affair with Philip Barton Key II, the son of Francis Scott Key, the writer of the national anthem. Sickles shot Key to death in broad daylight in Lafayette Park just yards from the White House. Sickles was subsequently acquitted with the very first temporary-insanity defense, thus establishing a legal precedent. The defense attorney representing Sickles was Edwin Stanton, the future secretary of war under Abraham Lincoln.

When the Civil War began in 1861, despite having no combat experience, Sickles secured the rank of Union major general through political connections. At the battle of Gettysburg Sickles disobeyed orders from his commander, General George Meade, by not taking up a defensive position at Cemetery Ridge. Instead, he proceeded with his troops to a terrain known as the Peach Orchard and stretched his men too thinly in a line vulnerable to an attack from all sides. The only thing that saved Sickles from a court martial afterward was the fact that he had most of his right leg blown off at Gettysburg. Sickles had the audacity to donate what remained of his mangled leg to the National Museum of Health and Medicine with a card that read, "With the Compliments of Major General D.E.S."

In 1893, long after the Civil War, Sickles was elected to the House of Representatives. Sickles then proceeded to introduce a piece of legislation awarding himself the Congressional Medal of Honor for his self-proclaimed heroics at the Battle of Gettysburg! The bill passed, and the citation was issued in 1897.

Sickles's lasting legacy was his work in the preservation of the Gettysburg battlefield. He sponsored legislation to form the Gettysburg National Military Park by buying up private lands and erecting monuments.

Sickles died in 1914, succumbing to a cerebral hemorrhage. His funeral was held at New York City's St. Patrick's Cathedral with then Cardinal John Farley officiating.

FUN FACT

Daniel Sickles played a major role in the disputed presidential election of 1876 between Rutherford B. Hayes and Samuel Tilden. When most of the votes had been counted, it appeared that the Democrat Tilden had defeated the Republican Hayes. Hayes actually went to bed on election night thinking he had lost. But Dan Sickles reviewed the various statewide Electoral College votes and telegraphed a Hayes operative, urging that Hayes contest the results in Oregon, Louisiana, Florida, and South Carolina. It took months for a presidential commission to finally award Hayes, who had lost the popular vote, all of the contested votes in the Electoral College, allowing Hayes to become president by a single vote.

DIRECTIONS

At Memorial Avenue take a right at Eisenhower Drive and proceed till you reach Bradley Drive. Turn right. At the next intersection take Porter Drive. Follow this approximately ¼ mile until you see a steep hill on your left. Climb the hill carefully, and you will find yourself on Miles Drive, which is flat. Walk about 50 feet to your left, and Sickles's stone is in the sixth row. You will recognize it by the fact that his Congressional Medal of Honor status affords him that lettering in gold leaf. Whew! And then congratulate yourself for finding this difficult-to-locate grave.

CHAPTER TWO

Mount Auburn Cemetery

580 MOUNT AUBURN STREET

CAMBRIDGE, MASSACHUSETTS 02138

Photo courtesy of Melissa Capuano

L ocated just a few miles from Boston, this Cambridge cemetery, founded in 1831, was designated a National Historic Landmark in 2003. In the early 19th century, as the population in the Boston area started to grow, there was a need for more burial sites, as well as a demand for better use of urban land. The founding of Mount Auburn in large part solved both of these needs. Inspired by the Père Lachaise Cemetery in Paris, Mount Auburn Cemetery was America's first land-scaped cemetery. The tranquility afforded by scenic grounds, inspiring architectural structures, and an array of flowers and plants quickly made Mount Auburn one of the our country's most popular tourist sites.

Open every day, this 175-acre cemetery remains popular, with estimated annual visitors of approximately 200,000.

HENRY WADSWORTH LONGFELLOW
Poet
Born: February 7, 1797
Died: March 24, 1882

One of us has always had an appreciation for Longfellow's skill with words, having studied him in college. Further research on Longfellow indicated an interesting and often sad life story.

Henry Wadsworth Longfellow was born in Portland, Maine, which at the time was part of the state of Massachusetts. At a very young age Longfellow demonstrated a love for both reading and writing. In his final year at Maine's Bowdoin College, Longfellow decided to pursue a career in literature. After graduation, he spent three years traveling through Europe to study the Romance languages. He became fluent in French, Italian, Spanish, and German. Longfellow's writings were much influenced by his time abroad and the various methods of European expression that he had studied. In fact, his critics argued that Longfellow's work imitated European verse and lacked originality.

Longfellow taught modern languages as a professor at both his alma mater, Bowdoin, and later at Harvard. He initially gained fame with two books of poetry, *Voices of the Night* in 1839 and *Ballads and Other Poems* in 1841. His epic poem "Evangeline," published in 1847, was immensely popular. Longfellow's popularity then achieved "rock

*Henry Wadsworth
Longfellow's Grave*
(Courtesy of
Melissa Capuano)

star" status through his later writings, such as *The Song of Hiawatha* in 1855 and *The Courtship of Miles Standish and Other Poems* in 1858. His poem "Paul Revere's Ride," more popularly known as "The Midnight Ride of Paul Revere," was published in 1861 and remains popular today.

Longfellow died in 1882 as the result of peritonitis. He is buried with his two wives (both lost under tragic circumstances) and other family members.

FUN FACTS

1. Longfellow's circle of friends included notables such as Nathaniel Hawthorne, Washington Irving, Ralph Waldo Emerson, Oliver Wendell Homes, Senator Charles Sumner of Civil War fame, and Edgar Allan Poe.
2. Longfellow and Edgar Allan Poe had a falling out, with Poe accusing Longfellow of plagiarism. Longfellow never responded to Poe's accusation, but following Poe's death Longfellow wrote, "The harshness of his criticisms, I have never attributed to anything but the irritation of a sensitive nature, chafed by some indefinite sense of wrong."

DIRECTIONS

Obtain a cemetery map from the cemetery office just within the entrance gate. Longfellow's is grave #36 on the map. From the main entrance gate, follow Central Avenue and take the first left onto Fountain Avenue. Look for Halcyon Avenue, which will be on the left, but do not turn down it. Directly across the street from Halcyon, you'll find the start of Catalpa Path. The path takes you up a slight incline. When you reach the intersection of Catalpa Path and Indian Ridge Path, you will find the Longfellow gravesite. The grave is set at the top of the ridge, technically on Indian Ridge Path, on the right-hand side.

EDWARD EVERETT
Politician/Orator
Born: April 11, 1794
Died: January 15, 1865

Virtually anyone associated with Abraham Lincoln is of interest to us. So when we are in Mount Auburn Cemetery, we make it a point to visit Edward Everett's resting place.

Edward Everett, who is best known as the speaker who spoke before Abraham Lincoln delivered his immortal Gettysburg Address, was born in Massachusetts. Though he is primarily remembered as an accomplished orator, the resume of the posts he held during his lifetime is impressive.

An extremely bright and well-read young man, he entered Harvard at the age of 13 and graduated with high honors. After college he entered divinity school, and just shy of his 20th birthday became a preacher. Though he became popular for his sermons, his ministry was brief as he was offered a professorship at Harvard to teach languages. Before accepting the position at Harvard, he studied abroad overseas, earning a Ph.D. from the University of Göttingen in Germany. Upon his return to the United States, he taught at Harvard, but was quickly dissatisfied with a career of teaching. In 1821 he left Harvard to become editor of the *North American Review*, a journal of politics and culture. His public speaking on issues of the day then led to his being elected to the House of Representatives in 1825. Subsequently he became governor of Massachusetts, ambassador to Great Britain, secretary of state, and a U.S. senator.

In 1860 he was the candidate of the Constitutional Union Party for Vice President, running on a ticket headed by John Bell. Abraham

Edward Everett's Grave (Courtesy of Melissa Capuano)

Lincoln won a narrow victory that November. In 1863, at the Gettysburg cemetery dedication, Everett was the featured speaker, delivering a 13,000-word speech. This contrasted with Lincoln's 271 words of the Gettysburg Address. The next day Everett wrote to Lincoln, "I should be glad, to flatter myself, that I came as near to the central idea for the occasion in two hours, as you did in two minutes."

Everett died in 1865, probably from pneumonia.

FUN FACT

Edward Everett played a very significant role in the preservation of George Washington's home at Mount Vernon. Everett toured the country giving speeches about Washington and raising funds for the preservation of Mount Vernon. Everett himself donated a good portion of the monies raised.

DIRECTIONS

Everett's grave is #18 on the map. Follow Fountain Avenue deep into the center of the cemetery. Fountain turns into Magnolia Avenue. Once you pass Swan Avenue on the left, you are getting close. As Magnolia Avenue starts a slight incline, you'll find the site of Edward Everett to the right. His grave is just before the turnoff to Mountain Avenue. It is set only slightly back from Magnolia Avenue, up on a small hill, and you should see the main tower in the background.

CHARLES SUMNER
U.S. Senator
Born: January 6, 1811
Died: March 11, 1874

As the chairman of the Senate Foreign Relations Committee, Charles Sumner was so powerful that both Abraham Lincoln and Ulysses Grant had to go out of their way "with hat in hand" to confer with him.

Charles Sumner was born in Boston, Massachusetts. Fiercely anti-slavery, Sumner led what were then called the Radical Republicans, and he did all he could to destroy and punish the Southern states'

Charles Sumner's Grave (Courtesy of Melissa Capuano)

Confederacy. Sumner thought Abraham Lincoln too moderate in his approach to the South. Sumner pressed for emancipation as soon as Lincoln assumed office.

Possessing a keen intellect, Sumner was also a fiery speaker who took a no-holds-barred approach, often addressing his colleagues in an insulting manner on the floor of the Senate. This was famously demonstrated in 1856 when Sumner, in a fierce antislavery speech, made sexual insinuations about a South Carolina senator. Two days after the speech, Sumner was attacked and nearly beaten to death by a cane-wielding relative of the insulted senator. It took about three years before Sumner recovered enough to return to the duties of the Senate, eventually becoming the powerful chairman of the Foreign Relations Committee.

In 1870 Sumner disagreed with President Ulysses Grant's plan to annex the Dominican Republic, and this led to an irreparable rift between the two men. Sumner opposed Grant's reelection in 1872, and Grant retaliated by using his influence to have Sumner removed from his Senate chairmanship.

Charles Sumner died of a heart attack in 1874.

DIRECTIONS

A short walk from the grave of Edward Everett lies Charles Sumner, in grave #59 on the map. Continue forward on Magnolia Avenue, past the turnoff to Mountain Avenue on your right. Magnolia turns into Walnut Avenue. On the left, keep an eye out for Arethusa Path. Only a few steps down the path you'll find the site of Charles Sumner on your left.

EDWIN BOOTH
Shakespearean Stage Actor
Born: March 13, 1833
Died: June 7, 1893

The stories involving Edwin Booth and his more notorious brother John Wilkes Booth are too delicious for us to bypass.

Born in Maryland, Edwin Booth was the illegitimate son of Junius Brutus Booth, an acclaimed and popular thespian. Edwin and his brothers followed their father's encouragement to become actors themselves. Today many theater historians rank Edwin Booth as one of the American theater's greatest performers. Edwin's signature role was Shakespeare's Hamlet, which he once performed for 101 consecutive performances. However, and unfortunately for Edwin, his theater legacy will always be overshadowed by the notoriety of his younger brother John Wilkes Booth, assassin of Abraham Lincoln.

Unlike his brother, Edwin Booth was a Union supporter and an abolitionist. Following the Lincoln assassination, Edwin disowned his younger brother. However, after petitioning President Andrew Johnson in 1869, he gained custody of his brother's remains and had his brother buried in an unmarked grave in the family plot in Baltimore, Maryland.

Edwin Booth died in 1893 as the result of a series of strokes.

Edwin Booth's Grave
(Courtesy of Melissa Capuano)

FUN FACT

In an ultimate irony Edwin Booth may have saved the life of, or at least prevented serious harm to, Robert Lincoln, the oldest son of Abraham Lincoln. A few months before the assassination, Robert Lincoln was at the Jersey City, New Jersey, train station. On a crowded platform he lost his footing and was in danger of falling down on the locomotive tracks as a train was starting to move. Edwin Booth grabbed Lincoln's collar and prevented the fall.

DIRECTIONS

Booth's grave is #7 on the map. From the grave of Sumner, continue forward on Walnut Avenue. The next left is Mound Avenue. At the intersection of Walnut and Mound, look for the start of Orange Path. Only a few steps down the path, you'll find the start of Anemone Path on your right. Take Anemone up the slight incline, and you should be overlooking Mound Avenue on your right. As you continue up the hill, you'll come to the site of Edwin Booth on your left toward the top of the incline.

CHAPTER THREE

Woodlawn Cemetery

EAST 233RD STREET AND WEBSTER AVENUE

BRONX, NEW YORK 10470

Photo courtesy of Joseph Connor

Designated a National Historic Landmark in 2011, this cemetery has often been described as an outdoor museum because of its impressive landscapes and structures. The cemetery encompasses more than 400 acres and is occupied by over 300,000 final resting places. The atmosphere resembles a park more than a cemetery. It was established in 1863 as the result of increased demand for residential and commercial real estate in the heart of New York City, and many graveyards in denser parts of the city had their dead disinterred and reinterred at Woodlawn. The first celebrity buried here was arguably Admiral David Farragut, who passed away in 1870. Today the graves of many other notables—politicians, musicians, entertainers, business figures, writers, and others—can be found at Woodlawn.

The cemetery is typically open every day from 8:30 a.m. to 4:30 p.m., though the office is closed on Sundays and major holidays. Woodlawn reserves the right to close the entire cemetery as the result of inclement weather.

DAVID FARRAGUT
Navy Admiral
Born: July 5, 1801
Died: August 14, 1870

Whenever the Civil War is discussed or read about, nearly everyone recognizes the names of army generals Ulysses Grant, William Sherman, Robert E. Lee, and Stonewall Jackson. However, ask anyone to name a naval officer associated with the Civil War and it is more likely you will draw a blank look.

A native son of Tennessee, David Farragut was introduced at an early age to the rigors of life at sea. Farragut's father operated a ferry in Tennessee and had been a naval lieutenant in the Revolutionary War. When Farragut's mother passed away, his father placed him in the foster care of David Porter, a Navy man himself. David Porter saw to it that his foster son was commissioned as a midshipman at age nine. At age eleven Farragut served under David Porter in the War of 1812.

David Farragut would spend his entire career in Navy service. He served as a commander during the Mexican-American War. Despite being born a Southerner and residing in Virginia at the outset of the

David Farragut's Grave (Courtesy of Joseph Connor)

Civil War, Farragut considered secession treasonous and sided with Union forces. After achieving naval victory in the Battle of New Orleans in 1862, he became the first American to achieve the rank of rear admiral. Two years later, after leading his fleet to another important victory in the Battle of Mobile Bay, Farragut was promoted by President Abraham Lincoln to vice admiral of the United States Navy. Following the war, Farragut reached the rank of full admiral.

David Farragut died in 1870 of a heart attack. The procession to his Woodlawn grave was two miles long and was headed by President Ulysses S. Grant.

FUN FACT

In the Battle of Mobile Bay, David Farragut is known for having said, "Damn the torpedoes. Full speed ahead!" However, that well-known quote is a paraphrase. He is actually credited with saying the much less catchy line, "Damn the torpedoes. Four bells Captain Drayton. Forward [Commander] Jouett. Full Speed!"

DIRECTIONS

Obtain a cemetery map from the cemetery office near the entrance. Farragut lies nearby in the Aurora Hill section. Take Central Avenue and make a left onto Ravine Avenue.

DUKE ELLINGTON

Band Leader/Composer/Pianist
Born: April 29, 1899
Died: May 24, 1974

Like most other people we love music. We appreciate all forms, from rock to classical. Jazz has a niche that is difficult to describe, but one thing is certain: it is uniquely American. There is no one, in our minds, who brought out the feel of jazz more than Duke Ellington.

Edward Kennedy Ellington was born in Washington, DC, to parents who were both pianists. Ellington's mother saw to it that he was taught proper manners and behaved in a dignified manner. His boyhood friends tagged him with the nickname Duke because of his graceful persona and dapper style of dress.

Duke Ellington's Grave
(Courtesy of Joseph Connor)

   In the early 20th century, ragtime music, a forerunner of jazz, was popular, and it very much influenced and inspired Ellington. At age 23 Ellington first appeared with his band in New York's Broadway nightclubs. Their distinct musical style fit in well in the era now called the "Roaring Twenties." Ellington demonstrated his genius in musical arrangement with hits such as "Mood Indigo" and "Reminiscing in Tempo" in the early 1930s. In 1932 he and his band began their legendary years at Harlem's famed Cotton Club. In 1939 Billy Strayhorn, a close associate of Ellington, wrote the song that quickly became Ellington's signature piece, "Take the 'A' Train."

After World War II, public taste in music shifted away from jazz, and Ellington's popularity started to wane. However, Ellington's tour of Europe during the early 1950s was very successful. In the mid 1950s there was a revival of appreciation for the Duke's music, which continued until he passed away in 1974 as the result of lung cancer.

DIRECTIONS

Obtain a map from the main office at the entrance of the cemetery. Ellington's grave is at the intersection of Fir Avenue, Heather Avenue, and Knollwood Avenue (Hillcrest, Alpine, Wild Rose, and Fir sections).

MILES DAVIS

Jazz Trumpeter
Born: May 26, 1926
Died: September 28, 1991

In the early days of jazz there were a number of superb trumpeters, such as Louis Armstrong and Dizzy Gillespie. But for us no one can match the interpretive skills of Miles Davis.

Miles Davis was born in Illinois to a middle-class family. His mother, a music teacher, encouraged him to be a violin player. However, Davis preferred the trumpet, and after graduating from high school he was allowed to sit in with Billy Eckstine's band, which featured Dizzy Gillespie on trumpet and Charlie Parker on saxophone. Those two legendary musicians' style of fast-paced bebop jazz greatly influenced Davis.

Yet Davis never felt constrained to stick to the same type of music. In the late 1940s his band developed a relaxed sound that came to be known as cool jazz. In 1959 Davis's album *Kind of Blue* was released, and it is now often considered the greatest jazz album of all time. As time progressed, Davis experimented with all types of music, including popular tunes and rock 'n' roll. Davis won six Grammy awards in his lifetime, plus a lifetime achievement award, and two more Grammys were awarded posthumously.

Despite his talent and fame, or perhaps because of them, Davis led a troubled personal life. He was divorced three times and battled alco-

Miles Davis's Tomb (Courtesy of Joseph Connor)

hol and drug abuse most of his life. He died at age 65 from complications arising from a stroke, pneumonia, and respiratory failure.

FUN FACT

Miles Davis earned the nickname "The Prince of Darkness" as the result of his aloofness on stage and his habit of turning his back on audiences.

DIRECTIONS

Same as for Duke Ellington.

LIONEL HAMPTON

Jazz Vibraphonist/Band Leader
Born: April 20, 1908
Died: August 31, 2002

Whenever we hear a Lionel Hampton record, it brings a smile to our faces. We find it difficult not to move to Hampton's skill with a vibraphone, whether it be snapping our fingers or tapping our feet.

Born in the Kentucky, Lionel Hampton was taught by a nun how to play the drums at Holy Rosary Academy near Chicago. Early in his career as a drummer, Hampton also learned the vibraphone. One evening Louis Armstrong heard Hampton play the vibes and later asked Hampton to join him in several songs. After studying music at the University of Southern California, Hampton formed his own band in 1934.

Lionel Hampton's Grave (Courtesy of Joseph Connor)

In 1936 Benny Goodman asked Hampton to join Goodman's small band. This marked the first racially integrated jazz band in the United States. In 1940 Hampton left Goodman's band and once again formed his own band. In 1942 Hampton recorded his signature song, "Flying Home," which he had cowritten with Goodman.

Though jazz's popularity declined in the late 1940s and early 1950s, Lionel Hampton remained popular with live audiences. He toured Europe several times and was enthusiastically received.

Hampton's ability to do live performances was drastically reduced by a stroke suffered in 1991. He died in 2002 as the result of heart failure.

FUN FACTS

1. In 1968 Hampton received a Papal Medal from Pope Paul VI.
2. To accommodate Hampton's wish to be buried as close as possible to Duke Ellington, Woodlawn Cemetery had to remove a shrub to create the gravesite for Lionel and his wife.

DIRECTIONS

Same as for Duke Ellington.

CHARLES EVANS HUGHES

Chief Justice of the Supreme Court
Born: April 11, 1862
Died: August 27, 1948

We love presidential election history, and the fact that Charles Evans Hughes came so excruciatingly close to getting elected president in 1916 makes him a person of interest to us.

Charles Evans Hughes was born in the state of New York. Other than president of the United States, what high public office didn't this man achieve? Always a very bright and intelligent student, Hughes graduated from Columbia Law School in 1884 with highest honors. Following his graduation, Hughes practiced law with a distinguished firm and taught law at New York University. In 1906, promoting progressive policies, Hughes was elected governor of New York, defeating media mogul William Randolph Hearst. In 1908 Hughes turned

down William Howard Taft's offer to be his running mate in the presidential election, choosing instead to run for reelection as governor.

In 1910 President Taft chose Hughes to fill a vacancy on the Supreme Court. The Senate quickly confirmed Hughes, but in 1916 Hughes resigned from the Court to accept the Republican Party's nomination for the presidency. Running against incumbent President Woodrow Wilson, Hughes lost an extremely close contest. In 1921 President Warren Harding chose Hughes to be his secretary of state.

Finally, in 1930, President Herbert Hoover picked Hughes to be the chief justice of the Supreme Court, following the death of his almost former running mate Chief Justice William Howard Taft. Hughes served as chief justice until his retirement in 1941.

Hughes died in 1948 from cancer.

FUN FACT

A shift of less than 2,000 votes in California in the presidential election of 1916 would have given Hughes the electoral votes to win the presidency. The loss of California is mostly attributed to Hughes's failure to keep an appointment with then Governor Hiram Johnson. Angry, the governor refused to lift a finger for Hughes in the presidential campaign.

DIRECTIONS

The grave is in the Elder Section on Elder Avenue near the corner of Prospect Avenue, after a water spigot. The grave marker is level with the ground, behind bushes.

BAT MASTERSON

Western Lawman/Journalist
Born: November 26, 1853
Died: October 25, 1921

As kids we loved the Gene Barry TV series *Bat Masterson*. When we got older, we read about the real Bat Masterson and found his life story intriguing.

Bartholomew William Barclay "Bat" Masterson was born in Canada but lived most of his childhood in upstate New York, working with his brothers on his family's farm. As a young man Masterson moved to the Midwest, where he worked at a variety of jobs, including buffalo hunter and Indian scout in Dodge City, Kansas. In 1877 Masterson was elected sheriff of Ford County, Kansas.

As a lawman, Masterson took part in well-publicized gunfights and arrests that involved Wild West legends like Wyatt Earp and Buffalo Bill Cody. However, controversy involving Masterson's role in a high-profile shooting caused him to leave Dodge City (get out of

Bat Masterson's Grave (Courtesy of Joseph Connor)

Dodge, as it were) in 1882. He eventually settled in Denver, Colorado, not as a lawman but as the operator of a gambling house. Masterson developed a passion for prizefighting, and this led him to operate a boxing club. He came to know all the heavyweight champions from John L. Sullivan to Jack Dempsey, attending virtually all the heavyweight championship bouts.

In 1902 Masterson moved to New York City and became a sportswriter for the *New York Telegraph*. In 1905 President Theodore Roosevelt appointed Masterson to be deputy U.S. marshal for the Southern District of New York. Masterson served in this position until 1909.

Masterson died of a massive heart attack at his desk at the *New York Telegraph* while writing what would be his final sports column.

DIRECTIONS

The grave is in the Primrose Section. Travel down Border Avenue and make a left onto Spiraea Avenue. With your back to the Reinhardt monument in the Spiraea Section, walk between the Gullery monument to your left and the Gallo monument to your right, toward the Jantzen monument. Bat Matterson is hidden behind the Jantzen monument.

ALEXANDER HERRMANN
Magician
Born: February 10, 1844
Died: December 17, 1896

Like most youngsters we were fascinated by magic tricks. This led to our initial interest in the life of the famed Harry Houdini. But Houdini was not America's first famous magician. In the 1800s magic acts were very popular in America. It is hard to refute that Alexander Herrmann was the most popular American magician before Houdini.

Alexander Herrmann was born into a family of magicians (both his father and eldest brother were performing magicians) in Paris, France. At a very young age Herrmann was mentored by his eldest brother in the art and skills of being a performer and magician. In time Herrmann became adept in the skill of sleight of hand. He wowed audiences with his card-throwing ability. Though Herrmann wore a pointy goatee and mustache, which gave him a dark look, he introduced humor into his act, and this added to his popularity.

As Herrmann's reputation grew, he toured both Europe and the Americas. In 1875 he married Adelaide Scarcez, who would become an integral part of his act, as well as his legacy. The following year, Herrmann became a naturalized citizen of the United States, and he settled in a mansion in Whitestone, Queens. On a world tour in 1882, the czar of Russia was so impressed and awed by Herrmann that he proclaimed him "Herrmann the Great."

Innovative as well as daring, Herrmann was constantly searching for new illusions to incorporate into his act. Late in his career he performed the dangerous "bullet catch" trick. The intended illusion here is that the magician catches a bullet in his mouth or hand from a pistol fired directly at him. When the pistol misfired, fatalities were known to have occurred. Consequently Herrmann's wife and assistant, Adelaide, could not bear to see her husband perform this trick.

Herrmann died on board a train from a heart attack. He was only 52.

Alexander and Adelaide Herrmann's Graves (Courtesy of Joseph Connor)

DIRECTIONS

Herrmann's grave is in the Oak Hill Section at the intersection of Prospect Avenue, Hawthorn Avenue, and Oakland Avenue. Look for the Prospect Avenue sign, then walk behind the sign. Herrmann's final resting place is behind the Koster monument.

ADELAIDE HERRMANN

Magician/Dancer/Bicyclist
Born: August 11, 1853
Died: February 19, 1932

Adelaide Herrmann was the first female magician of major note and holds a unique place in American entertainment history.

Adelaide Scarcez was born in London, England. Little is known of her early life. She came to America at age 22 as a trained dancer. In

1874, after her second encounter with magician Alexander Herrmann, Adelaide agreed to his marriage proposal. Adelaide Herrmann became a very important part of her husband's career. She was his assistant on stage and often entertained audiences with dances or bicycle tricks when Alexander needed a break between his routines.

When Alexander died suddenly in 1896, Adelaide continued her husband's act. Female magicians were a rarity, and she was certainly the first woman in this country to achieve a high level of success in the field. Adelaide Herrmann was eventually billed as the "Queen of Magic." Ironically, despite Adelaide's inability to watch her husband perform the dangerous "bullet catch" trick, she adopted this illusion in her own act.

Adelaide Herrmann continued her career in magic until she retired in 1926. She passed away in 1929 and is buried next to her husband.

FUN FACT

In 2010 Adelaide Herrmann's descendants discovered her written memoirs, and in 2012—more than 80 years after her passing—they were published.

DIRECTIONS

Same as for Alexander Herrmann.

NORA BAYES
Entertainer
Born: October 3, 1880
Died: March 19, 1928

Like most youngsters we enjoyed watching the glorious films of Laurel and Hardy on TV. One of their movies, *The Flying Deuces*, made in 1939, has an endearing scene with Oliver Hardy singing a song that is still recognizable today: "Shine On, Harvest Moon." While Ollie sings, Stan Laurel dances. The scene concludes with Laurel and Hardy doing a soft-shoe dance together. When the *New York Times* reported in April 2018 that the cowriter of "Shine On, Harvest Moon" was a huge star in her day, and that she had to wait 90 years for a headstone

Nora Bayes's Grave

for her grave, we became intrigued. Research into that star's life compelled us to include her in this volume.

Born as Rachel Eleanora Goldberg to a Jewish Orthodox family in Chicago, Nora Bayes was to many the greatest star of the vaudeville and Broadway stages in the first quarter of the 20th century. Bayes's talents extended to her being a singer, actress, comedian, and composer.

Bayes co-wrote "Shine On, Harvest Moon" with her second husband, Jack Norworth, who was himself a singer and songwriter. Norworth wrote the baseball standard "Take Me Out to the Ball Game," and Nora Bayes was the first to sing it on stage.

In 1917 legendary Broadway composer George M. Cohan, in response to America's entry into World War I, wrote the patriotic song "Over There" and asked Nora Bayes to record it. The song became an international hit. Although known as a prima donna, Bayes was actively involved in entertaining U.S. troops during the war, and rightly earned the nation's gratitude.

Bayes was only 48 years old when she died in 1928 from intestinal cancer.

Bayes's death led to a strange saga. Her fifth husband, businessman Benjamin Friedland, had her remains stored in Woodlawn Cemetery's receiving vault for 18 years for unknown reasons. Friedland later remarried, and when he passed away in 1946, his second wife bought a plot at Woodlawn and had both her husband and Nora Bayes interred there. The graves were left unmarked for again-unknown reasons. The second Mrs. Friedland died years later and was cremated elsewhere. After several years of prodding from one of Nora Bayes's fans, Woodlawn finally secured permission from a relative of the second Mrs. Friedland and placed markers on the graves of Bayes and Friedland. In April 2018 a ceremony was held to unveil the markers, and after 90 years Nora Bayes had a visible resting place.

FUN FACTS

1. Nora Bayes was known to have wired vaudeville producer Edward Albee stating, "Beginning next week my salary must be $10,000 per week." This was a marked increase from her current salary of $1,000 per week. Albee promptly refused. At her next performance she sang eight bars of her opening song, stopped, and said, "That's $1,000 of my act." She then proceeded to walk off.

2. She had little tolerance for coughing from an audience. When that would happen, she would feign a coughing spell and then say sarcastically, "Please excuse my very rude behavior."

DIRECTIONS

From Webster Avenue entrance continue on Central Avenue. Make a left on Myosotis Avenue. Follow Myosotis Avenue to the Sassafras Plot. Two rows in from Myosotis Avenue and Wintergreen Avenue.

NELLIE BLY

Reporter/Writer
Born: May 5, 1864
Died: January 27, 1922

Nellie Bly fits the profile of a Grave Tripper favorite very well. We feel it is a shame that she is not as well remembered today as she deserves to be. Bly's contributions were in the field of investigative journalism.

When on assignment, she demonstrated considerable courage, and her reporting often led to needed reforms.

Nellie Bly was born as Elizabeth Jane Cochran in Cochran Mills, Pennsylvania. Her father died when she was young, and shortly thereafter her mother moved Elizabeth and her siblings to Pittsburgh. In 1880 Elizabeth Cochran read a newspaper article in the *Pittsburgh Dispatch* titled "What Good Girls Are Good For," which implied that women were good only for giving birth and taking care of the house. Elizabeth wrote a response using the pseudonym "Little Orphan Girl." The editor of the newspaper was so impressed by the writing that he

Nellie Bly's Grave

asked, through ads in the *Dispatch*, that the writer come forward and identify herself. When she did, the editor asked her to write an article, under the same pseudonym, about how divorce affects women. The editor was then so pleased with the article that he offered her a permanent job, which she accepted, and she chose the pen name of Nellie Bly going forward. By 1887 Nellie Bly needed something more challenging than the arts and theater stories she was typically assigned. Bly left Pittsburgh for New York City, where Joseph Pulitzer of the *New York World* gave her the assignment of an undercover investigative exposé at the Women's Lunatic Asylum on Blackwell's Island (now known as Roosevelt Island). To investigate reports of brutality toward the inmates, she feigned insanity and had herself admitted. After ten days the *New York World* sent an attorney to the asylum to arrange for her release. Her findings, later published in the book *Ten Days in a Mad-House*, prompted many reforms in addition to giving her instant fame.

In 1888 Bly set out to go around the world in 80 days to emulate the Jules Verne novel. Traveling with only the clothes she had on, plus some undergarments and toiletries in a single travel bag, she set off on November 14, 1889. Despite pitfalls along the way Nellie Bly returned on January 25, 1890, having completed her global adventure in just 72 days.

In 1895 Bly married industrialist Robert Seaman. She was 31 years of age and he was 73. As the result of her husband's poor health, Bly retired from journalism. When Robert Seaman passed away in 1904, she assumed control of Iron Clad Manufacturing Company. It ultimately went bankrupt, and Bly returned to reporting.

Nellie Bly died of pneumonia at St. Mark's Hospital in New York City. She was interred in an unmarked grave until 1978 when the New York Press Club erected a monument to recognize her journalistic accomplishments.

DIRECTIONS

From the Webster Avenue entrance, continue on Central Avenue. Make a left on West Border Avenue. Follow West Border Avenue to the Honeysuckle plot on the right. Nellie's tombstone is clearly visible since it is upright in a sea of flat grave markers.

ELIZABETH CADY STANTON
Women's Suffrage Leader
Born: November 12, 1815
Died: October 26, 1902

One of our aunts, who had immigrated to the United States in the 1940s, told us that the labor union for garment workers that she had joined provided its female members with pamphlets and booklets covering the history of the women's suffrage movement. Our aunt told us that after reading about Elizabeth Stanton, one of the early leaders in the movement, she had come to admire her. This led us to our own research on Stanton and the wish to visit her gravesite.

Elizabeth Cady Stanton was born in Johnstown, New York. Her father, Daniel Cady, was an attorney who served a single term in the U.S. House of Representatives.

As a young child Elizabeth enjoyed reading her father's law books. It was through her interest in law that she saw how the legal scales favored men over women. She felt the pains of discrimination herself when she was barred from attending Union College, which accepted men with academic standings far less impressive than hers.

Stanton's active involvement in the women's suffrage movement started in 1848, when she and other like-minded women, such as Lucretia Mott and Jane Hunt, organized the Seneca Falls Convention in northern New York State. At the convention Stanton drafted a Declaration of Sentiments, which in essence proclaimed that men and women were equal and took the then-radical position that women should have the right to vote.

Stanton met Susan B. Anthony in 1851, and they initially worked together in the temperance movement. It was Stanton's opinion that drunkenness would be sufficient cause for divorce. On behalf of women's suffrage they made an effective team. Stanton was the better speaker and writer, while Anthony was the better organizer and tactician. Though both were abolitionists on the slavery issue, Stanton and Anthony lobbied strongly against the 14th and 15th Amendments to the U.S. Constitution, which recognized the citizenship and the right to vote of former slaves. By not including women, Stanton and Anthony felt, the amendments were discriminatory and unacceptable.

Elizabeth Cady Stanton's Grave

Stanton went on to write or coauthor many influential books, such as the six-volume *History of Woman Suffrage*, whose early volumes were published in 1881 and 1886, and *The Woman's Bible*, published in 1895 and 1898. In 1892 she addressed the issue of suffrage before the U.S. House Committee on the Judiciary.

She died of heart failure in 1902, 18 years before women were finally permitted to vote.

DIRECTIONS

The gravesite is in the Lake Plot, Section 48, Lots 5421–5859. From the Webster Avenue Administration Office, take Central Avenue to just past the intersection of Lake Avenue. The Lake Plot is on the right-hand side, between Lake and Observatory Avenues. The Stanton gravesite is five spaces in from Observatory Avenue.

CHAPTER FOUR

Green–Wood Cemetery

500 25TH STREET EAST

BROOKLYN, NEW YORK 11232

Photo courtesy of Joseph Connor

Founded in 1838, Green-Wood Cemetery, like many of the other cemeteries of this era, was established largely because of overcrowding in local church graveyards. This property, previously farmland, was chosen for its beautiful vistas, rolling hills, and winding roads. It soon became a popular hangout for family outings and picnics. In the second half of the 19th century, Green-Wood's topography, statues, chapel, and other structures, such as the memorial obelisk near the cemetery's entrance, made it the second most popular tourist spot in the country after Niagara Falls.

This cemetery's 478 acres served as the inspiration for New York City's Central and Prospect Parks. In 2006, like its nearby Bronx neighbor Woodlawn Cemetery, Green-Wood was designated a National Historic Landmark.

Green-Wood Cemetery's main entrance is open from 8 a.m. to 5 p.m. from October through March. The hours from April through September are 7 a.m. to 7 p.m.

BOSS TWEED
Politician/Local Democratic Party Leader
Born: April 3, 1823
Died: April 12, 1878

Being residents of New York City, we have found the city's local history to be rich in significant and influential "good guys" and "bad guys." In the latter category this "gentleman" ranks toward the top of the list.

William Magear "Boss" Tweed was born in New York City. His name and that of Tammany Hall, the New York City Democratic Party machine, will forever be synonymous with crooked politics. Originally known as the Society of St. Tammany, Tammany Hall came into existence in 1854 with the election of corrupt New York City Mayor Fernando Wood. It was officially dissolved in 1867. Tammany Hall put Tweed up as a candidate for various offices, including local alderman, the U.S. House of Representatives, and the New York State Senate. In these offices Tweed became adept at advancing his career through graft and bribery.

As a member of the New York County Board of Supervisors,

Boss Tweed's Grave (Courtesy of Joseph Connor)

which oversaw the operations of the county government, Tweed lined his own pockets as well as those of his associates. This was accomplished by forcing vendors to pay an "overcharge" (a nicer word for bribe) to do business in the city. Tweed also supplemented his income by purchasing a printing company and seeing to it that it became the official printer of the City of New York, responsible for the printing of official documents, forms, financial statements, and such. Anyone making use of the city's printer would be charged a fee that far exceeded the cost. With allies in the offices of mayor and city controller, Tweed and his cohorts in Tammany Hall defrauded taxpayers of millions of dollars through city projects involving construction and development.

The *New York Times* in 1871 published the records of Tweed's recently deceased bookkeeper, providing evidence of Tammany Hall's defrauding of New York City taxpayers. Shortly after the release of this news, Tweed was arrested, tried, and convicted of 204 criminal counts of corruption. He served only one year in prison. Shortly after he was released from federal prison, New York State brought civil charges against Tweed in an attempt to retrieve the fortune he had accumulated at the expense of New York City. Tweed escaped from America to Spain. He was eventually located and brought back for trial in New York. Tweed died in jail in 1878 as the result of pneumonia.

FUN FACT

Boss Tweed may have been a crook, but at least you could never accuse him of thinking small. It has been estimated that Tweed stole anywhere from three million to 20 million dollars from New York City. In today's money that would be between 30 million and 200 million.

DIRECTIONS

We recommend that you get both the cemetery map and the cemetery guide at the office at the gate when you enter. The grave is in Section 55, Lot 6447, on Locust Avenue before Southwood Avenue. Look for it on the left-hand side, below Mossy Path (at about 8th Avenue on the 37th Street side). The Tweed family plot faces Locust.

LOLA MONTEZ

Entertainer/Courtesan
Born: February 17, 1821
Died: January 17, 1861

Perhaps the most famous of all courtesans, Lola Montez has been the subject of books and has been portrayed in a number of films.

Lola Montez was born Eliza Rosanna Gilbert in Ireland. During her spoiled childhood she exhibited a wild streak and a temper, which landed her in trouble in the various schools she attended. She married at age 16, and after separating from her husband five years later, she became a professional dancer. "Lola Montez the Spanish Dancer" was born.

A number of affairs with wealthy men earned her the reputation of being a courtesan. Montez eventually settled for a time in Paris, where she had an affair with Hungarian composer Franz Liszt, and possibly another with novelist Alexandre Dumas. She traveled to Munich in 1846, and met the man with whom she would have her most famous

affair: King Ludwig I of Bavaria. He awarded Montez the title of countess, and with it came political power. In 1848 revolutionary forces forced Ludwig to abdicate, and Montez escaped to Switzerland. After a scandalous marriage to a military officer in London, Montez came to the United States in 1851. Her performances as an actress in an autobiographical play titled "Lola Montez in Bavaria" drew rave reviews and large audiences. After marrying a newspaper reporter in 1853, she moved to California.

In 1855 Montez toured Australia and introduced a new number called "Spider Dance," which was criticized for its "low level of morality." During her new erotic number, it was recorded, she lifted her skirts to the point that the audience could see she was not wearing any undergarments. She returned to the United States in 1856 and in her final years became, of all things, a moral lecturer.

She died one month before her 40th birthday in 1861 as the result of syphilis.

FUN FACT

The premise of Montez's erotic "Spider Dance" was that spiders were crawling all over her. Her props were fake spiders she made out of cork.

DIRECTIONS

The grave is in Section 8, Lot 12730, on Summit Avenue, on the 37th Street side below 9th Avenue. From the intersection of Summit and Dale Avenues, walk past the Alpine Path sign, then past the Alpine Hill sign. On your left you'll pass the Vita headstone and the Anderson headstone. Next is Eliza Gilbert. See the back of the headstone for Lola Montez.

SAMUEL MORSE

Painter/Inventor
Born: April 27, 1791
Born: April 2, 1872

A fine painter and a groundbreaking inventor, Samuel Morse was truly unique in his talents.

Samuel Morse, born in Massachusetts, was primarily a painter by profession, but is best remembered as the inventor of the telegraph. The son of a Calvinist preacher, Morse attended Yale University, where he studied religious philosophy. While there, he showed an interest in science, particularly the relatively new study of electricity. However, after graduation Morse decided on a career in painting. In 1811 he traveled to England to study at the Royal Academy. Morse returned to the United States in 1815.

Early in his career, Morse found work primarily doing portraits. He was a patriot, however, and yearned to make a work of art that expressed the American spirit. In 1821 he traveled to Washington, DC, and decided to paint the House of Representatives. This massive painting, which took three years to complete, depicts the architecture of the Old House Chamber, as well as 80 individuals. In 1831 Morse traveled to Paris, where he worked on his other masterpiece, *The Gallery of the Louvre*. His miniature representations of other famous works of art in that painting are exquisite. The painting includes the works of da Vinci, Caravaggio, Reni, and Vernet.

Samuel Morse's Grave
(Courtesy of Joseph Connor)

Morse did not invent the very first telegraph, but his was the first electromagnetic telegraph. Prior telegraphs were visual in nature, requiring someone present to see the signals and translate the received coded messages; the systems involved white and black panels, clocks, and telescopes. The electrically operated telegraph, demonstrated for the first time in 1838, was revolutionary. People and businesses could now communicate over long distances using electricity transmitted through wires. The coded messages employed what became known as Morse code. With the country growing rapidly, largely because of expanding railway lines, the invention of the electromagnetic telegraph could hardly have been more timely. In 1845 the Magnetic Telegraph Company was formed to build lines along the East Coast.

Morse died of pneumonia in 1872. He died a rich man, mostly as a result of his invention of the telegraph.

FUN FACT

Samuel Morse ran for mayor of New York City in 1836 on an anti-immigration and anti-Catholic platform. He received a grand total of 1,496 votes.

DIRECTIONS

The grave is in Section 32/25, Lot 5761, on top of a hill above Orchard Avenue on the 37th Street side. It is between 7th Avenue and 8th Avenue but closer to 8th Avenue. From the corner of Chapel Avenue and Orchard Avenue (you'll see the High-Wood Hill sign), walk on Orchard to the third set of stairs on the left. Look up to see the monument in brown stone with marble columns.

DEWITT CLINTON

Governor/Mayor/U.S. Senator
Born: March 2, 1769
Died: February 11, 1828

DeWitt Clinton nearly became president of the United States, and his accomplishments in public office are worthy of mention in this book.

DeWitt Clinton was born in Little Britain, New York, an area in the town of New Windsor in Orange County. Many local historians rank Clinton among the best governors and mayors New York has ever had. As the nephew of New York Governor George Clinton, DeWitt Clinton was first introduced to politics when he worked as his uncle's secretary after graduating from Columbia University. Having been a member of both the New York State Assembly and New York State Senate, he was selected to serve in the U.S. Senate for the remainder of a term when a vacancy arose in 1802. Clinton's tenure in the Senate was brief; he resigned after less than two years because he found the work unsatisfying.

He was appointed by the governor of New York State to his first of three terms as mayor of New York City in 1803. Back then, mayors were not elected by the citizens of the city. His final term ended in 1815. As mayor, Clinton founded the New York Historical Society and worked at improving sanitation in the city. In addition, Clinton

DeWitt Clinton's Grave
(Courtesy of Joseph Connor)

helped create an asylum for orphans, and years before the British invasion during the War of 1812, he fortified New York's harbors.

In 1812, when he was lieutenant governor of New York, Clinton ran as the presidential candidate of the soon-to-be-defunct Federalist Party. He lost narrowly to James Madison. In 1817 Clinton was elected to his first term as governor of New York State. His greatest achievement as governor was getting approval in 1817 for the construction of the Erie Canal, which was finished in 1825. The canal extended from the eastern shore of Lake Erie to the upper Hudson River, connecting New York City to the Great Lakes. The canal led to an economic boom as freight and passenger traffic to New York soared. Clinton deservedly was hailed, domestically and internationally, for his achievement in bringing the concept of the canal to fruition.

Governor Clinton passed away suddenly in 1828, most likely as the result of a heart attack.

FUN FACT

Abraham Lincoln's secretary of state, William Seward, was not the first man to be mocked derisively with a tagline. Just as Seward's proposed purchase of Alaska was dubbed "Seward's Folly," critics of the Erie Canal labeled Clinton's initial efforts as "Clinton's Folly" and "Clinton's Big Ditch."

DIRECTIONS

The gravesite is in Section 108, Lot 15478, on the 23rd Street side between 6th and 7th Avenues. From Battle Avenue, make a right on Bay Side Avenue. Then make the first left onto Bay Side Circle. Behind the Bay Side–Dell sign is the massive Clinton monument.

HORACE GREELEY

Newspaper Publisher/Editor
Born: February 3, 1811
Died: November 29, 1872

Horace Greeley was certainly a mover and shaker in the mid-1800s.

Born in Vermont, Greeley was an excellent student, a voracious reader, and had an amazing memory for detail. At age 15 he apprenticed with a printer and learned the rudiments of the printing business. At age 21 Greeley moved to New York City, and after several years he and a financial partner founded the magazine *The New-Yorker*. Greeley, as a contributor, was noted for his sharp political commentary.

In 1841 Greeley founded *The Tribune* with the ambitious intention of making it a nationally read newspaper. As editor, Greeley voiced his strong opposition to slavery and his support for the principles of the Whig Party. *The Tribune* became known for its detailed and substantive reporting. In time, Greeley's editorials did much to mold public opinion regarding a variety of issues, including slavery and government corruption.

With the demise of the Whig Party, Greeley became a Republican and a Lincoln supporter. Greeley often supported Lincoln's policies during the Civil War. However, Greeley was also critical of Lincoln's slowness to act, particularly on the issue of ending slavery. In 1872 Greeley accepted the nomination of a new Liberal Republican Party to oppose President Grant's reelection. Greeley also received the Democratic Party's nomination for President. In a contentious campaign, Greeley was soundly beaten.

Exhausted from his presidential campaign, and distraught over the loss of his wife, who had passed away shortly before the election, Horace Greeley died on November 29, 1872, just weeks after his defeat.

FUN FACT

Had Greeley won the 1872 presidential election, he would have been dead before he could be sworn in as president.

DIRECTIONS

The grave is in Section 35, Lot 2344, on the 36th Street side between 6th and 7th Avenues. It is on Oak Avenue between Landscape Avenue and Hillock Avenue, off Acacia Path. Make a right onto Oak from Landscape Avenue. You will find Greeley's site on the right-hand side, at the top of the hill; look for the green/blue bust on top of the base.

Horace Greeley's Grave
(Courtesy of Joseph Connor)

LAURA KEENE

Actress/Theater Manager
Born: July 20, 1826
Died: November 4, 1873

Being unapologetic Lincoln aficionados, we could not leave out the curious story regarding what happened at Ford's Theatre minutes after Lincoln was shot.

Laura Keene was a renowned and famous theater actress. She is also credited with being the first female theater manager of major stature and clout. Unfortunately, that is not what Keene is most remembered for. Today, her notoriety is attributed to the claim that very shortly after Abraham Lincoln was shot in Ford's Theatre, Keene entered the presidential box where the mortally wounded president lay and cradled his bleeding head in her arms.

Mary Jess Moss, who later took the stage name Laura Keene, was born in Winchester, England. Keene made her theatrical debut in London in 1851, where she caught the eye of an American theater manager who invited her to join his stock company (an organization of actors

Laura Keene's Grave (Courtesy of Joseph Connor)

typically assigned to one theater). After moving to the United States, Keene became not only a popular actress but also a theater manager, showing her genius for publicity. In an historical irony, it has been said that Keene had a brief affair with Edwin Booth, John Wilkes Booth's brother.

There are contradictory eyewitness accounts as to whether the legend of Keene holding the dying Lincoln's head is true. Was she there or was she not? As Hamlet might have said, that is the question.

Laura Keene died in 1873 at the young age of 47 as the result of tuberculosis.

DIRECTIONS

Take the eastern entrance on the Hamilton Parkway and turn left on Border Avenue. Go past Sassafras Avenue until you get to Corylus Path. Cross Corylus Path to Dale Avenue, and approximately 20 feet to the right you will find Laura Keene's grave with a cross-shaped tombstone.

CHAPTER FIVE

Hollywood Cemetery

412 SOUTH CHERRY STREET

RICHMOND, VIRGINIA 23220

Photo courtesy of Hollywood Cemetery

A picturesque cemetery noted for its hillsides and variety of trees, Hollywood Cemetery is the second most visited cemetery in the country after Arlington Cemetery. Founded in 1847, this cemetery overlooking the James River was the brainchild of two of its four founders, Joshua Fry and William Haxall, who were impressed by the grandeur of Mount Auburn Cemetery near Boston. Upon their return to Richmond, they resolved that a similar garden-style cemetery for Richmond needed to be established. The name "Hollywood" came from the large number of holly trees that surrounded the original 42 acres of property. Today Hollywood Cemetery encompasses 130 acres. Many Confederate soldiers are buried here, and in 1869 a 90-foot pyramid of dry-laid granite stones (no mortar was applied) was created as a memorial to the Confederate fallen. That pyramid, still in place, makes for impressive viewing.

In addition to containing the final resting places of two U.S. presidents as well as other notables, this cemetery has some very unusual graves. One features an "Iron Dog" statue of a Newfoundland dog standing over the grave of a three-year-girl by the name of Bernadine Rees. Legend has it that passersby have heard this dog growl as it protects the grave. Another unusual gravesite is the Lloyd Family plot, which contains the graves of a mother and father and their six children with tombstones in the shape of tree trunks.

Iron Dog Grave Ornament (Courtesy of Hollywood Cemetery)

Gravestones Shaped like Tree Trunks (Courtesy of Hollywood Cemetery)

Cemetery hours are from 8 a.m. to 5 p.m. The front office is open Monday through Friday from 8:30 a.m. to 4:30 p.m. Tours are available.

JAMES MONROE

U.S. President
Born: April 28, 1758
Died: July 4, 1831

Like Charles Evans Hughes, discussed in the Woodlawn chapter, what public post did James Monroe, a native Virginian, not hold? Unlike Hughes, James Monroe did become president of the United States.

Monroe's resume includes U.S. Senator, ambassador to the United Kingdom, ambassador to France, governor of Virginia, secretary of state, and secretary of war. The latter two posts were held in the James Madison administration.

At the age of 16, James Monroe entered the College of William and Mary in Williamsburg, Virginia. After just two years, he quit college in 1776 to enter the Continental Army in the battle for independence from Great Britain. With the rank of captain, Monroe was with General George Washington at Valley Forge. Later during the war, Monroe returned to Williamsburg to study law, met Thomas Jefferson, and became his political protégé. After the war Monroe became a delegate to the Virginia State Assembly, and later a representative in the Congress established by the Articles of Confederation.

In 1790, a year after the U.S. Constitution was ratified, Monroe was elected to the U.S. Senate. From 1794 to 1796 he served as ambassador to France. In 1799 he was elected governor of Virginia and served a three-year term. In 1802 Monroe joined the Jefferson administration. As an experienced foreign diplomat, he played an important

James Monroe's Grave (Courtesy of Hollywood Cemetery)

role in 1803 in negotiating the Louisiana Purchase, which doubled the size of the young nation. In that same year he became ambassador to the United Kingdom. When James Madison entered the White House in 1809, he initially chose Monroe to be his secretary of state and then later his secretary of war.

In 1816 Monroe was elected U.S. president and served two terms. His biggest accomplishment was the issuance of what is now known as the Monroe Doctrine in 1823. At that time, there was a fear that Spain would attempt to recolonize South America. The Monroe Doctrine, in essence, forbids any European country from colonization in North, Central, or South America, noting that any such attempt will be met with American resistance.

On the Fourth of July, 1831, James Monroe passed away as the result of tuberculosis and congestive heart disease. The unusual visual nature of Monroe's grave deserves mention. Monroe's above-ground sarcophagus is surrounded by a canopy-like iron cage, which has been nicknamed "The Birdcage." This structure has been recently renovated.

FUN FACT

In 1823 President Monroe rejected the foreign policy advice of former presidents Thomas Jefferson and James Madison, who urged him to form an alliance with Great Britain when Spain's apparent interest in recolonizing South America became a concern. Monroe instead followed the advice of Secretary of State John Quincy Adams, who was opposed to granting Great Britain any say in America's foreign policy. Monroe later wrote that his decision was also influenced by the admonition in George Washington's farewell address about not forming foreign alliances.

DIRECTIONS

From the main entrance proceed to Hollywood Avenue. At the intersection bear left onto Eastvale Avenue. Follow Eastvale to the intersection of Midvale and Waterview Avenue and take Waterview. Proceed on Waterview past Eliptic Avenue. About 100 feet on the right you will see the Mount Section, which is known as Presidents Circle. Monroe's birdcage-like tomb is the centerpiece and clearly visible.

JOHN TYLER

U.S. President/U.S. Senator/Governor
Born: March 29, 1790
Died: January 18, 1862

Nearly every student of United States history is familiar with the 1840 presidential campaign slogan "Tippecanoe and Tyler Too." Our tenth president, John Tyler is the Tyler of that slogan. Most presidential historians have not been kind to Tyler in their rankings of our presidents. Historians' disdain for Tyler is largely based on his support of slavery and his siding with the Confederacy during the Civil War. Most Americans know very little about him. However, John Tyler set important precedents regarding presidential succession that remain in effect today.

Born in Virginia, John Tyler attended the College of William and Mary. After completion of his studies, Tyler went on to study law and subsequently opened up his own law practice. In 1811, at age 21, Tyler began his political career by being elected to Virginia's House of Del-

John Tyler's Grave

egates. In 1816, running on a strong states' rights platform, he was elected to the U.S. House of Representatives. After a return to state politics, in 1825 Tyler was elected governor of Virginia. In less than two years he was selected to serve as one of his state's U.S. senators.

Tyler often disagreed with Democratic Party leadership. In 1836 he resigned from his Senate seat out of disagreement with a bill threatening military action against any state that violated a federal law regarding tariffs on imported goods. In 1840 the relatively new Whig Party nominated Tyler for vice president as the running mate of William Henry Harrison (the Tippecanoe of "Tippecanoe and Tyler Too"— Harrison had led U.S. troops to victory at the Battle of Tippecanoe). The Whig ticket was elected that November.

Tyler's tenure as vice president was very brief: Harrison died just one month after being sworn into office (making Harrison's presidential term the shortest ever). This marked the first time a president had died in office. The Constitution was a bit sketchy about the transfer of power, stating that when a president died or was removed from office, his powers and duties would be given to the vice president. Many at the time interpreted this to mean that the successor would serve as an acting or caretaker president and would continue to be known as "vice president." Tyler, however, insisted he was the president of the United States and had a judge administer the presidential Oath of Office to him. We still follow this precedent of presidential succession today.

Tyler bickered with the Whig Party leadership (do you see a pattern here?) and was not nominated for president in 1844. Years later, Tyler sided with the South on the issue of secession and at the start of the Civil War was elected to the Confederate Congress.

John Tyler died in 1862 as the result of a stroke. Confederate President Jefferson Davis saw to it that Tyler was given a Virginia state funeral with his burial at Hollywood Cemetery.

FUN FACTS

1. Because of the circumstances of his elevation to the office of president, his detractors referred to him as "His Accidency."
2. John Tyler was the first president to have impeachment proceedings begun against him (do you see the pattern now?).

DIRECTIONS
Same directions as to James Monroe. Tyler's monument is closer to
Waterview Avenue within the Presidents Circle.

JEFFERSON DAVIS
Confederate President
Born: June 3, 1808
Died: December 6, 1889

Though Jefferson Davis is hardly one of our favorite American historical figures, there is no denying that he played a significant role when
our nation was at war with itself. The contrast of Davis to Lincoln is
stark and ironic. The irony is that, at the start of the war, Lincoln's
decisions and leadership were strong and focused, but he was burdened
with a series of poor generals. Davis, on the other hand, had a number
of great generals, but his leadership of the Confederacy was weak.

Born in the Kentucky, Jefferson Davis came from a well-to-do
family. An unexceptional though adequate student, he graduated from
the U.S. Military Academy in 1828. Davis then went on to serve in the
Army with the rank of lieutenant.

In 1835, shortly after his wedding to his first wife, Sarah, Davis
resigned from the military to move to Mississippi and run his own
plantation. In 1840 Davis became involved in politics when he was
selected as a delegate to the Democratic Party's state convention. He
played a major role in Mississippi in helping to elect James Polk as
president. In 1846 he raised a volunteer regiment and served as its colonel in the Mexican–American War. In 1847 he was selected to serve the
remaining term of a U.S. senator who had passed away. In 1853 President Franklin Pierce chose Davis as his secretary of war. When Pierce's
term ended, Davis returned to his Mississippi plantation and reclaimed
his U.S. Senate seat.

Davis was a firm believer in a state's right to secede from the Union
if it so wished. In 1861, when Mississippi voted to secede, Davis resigned his Senate seat and was soon chosen to be president of the Confederate States. Historians generally do not rate Davis's performance as
Confederate president well. He is criticized for stretching the South's
military resources too thin, as he assigned almost equal weight and

Jefferson Davis's Grave

priority to the defense of all areas of the South. His overall strategy during the Civil War can be interpreted as defensive, with the goal of surviving to fight another day. Shortly after the war ended, Davis was captured and imprisoned for two years before being released on bail. Davis was never subject to a trial as a result of President Andrew Johnson's 1868 Christmas Day pardon for all participants in the Southern rebellion.

After the pardon, Davis survived for an additional 21 years, dying in 1889 as the result of complications from acute bronchitis and malaria.

FUN FACTS

1. Davis, as a young second lieutenant stationed in the Michigan territories, met and fell in love with his first wife, Sarah Knox Taylor. They were married in June 1835. She was the daughter of his first commander and future president of the United States, Zachary Taylor. Unfortunately, just months after their marriage, Sarah died as the result of either malaria or yellow fever.

2. Davis's second wife, Varina Banks Howell, whom he married in 1845, became, after Davis's death, a columnist for the *New York World* newspaper under editor Joseph Pulitzer.

DIRECTIONS

From the main entrance proceed to Hollywood Avenue. At the intersection bear left onto Eastvale Avenue. Follow Eastvale to the intersection of Midvale and Waterview. Stay left on Waterview and proceed to the end at the Davis Circle. Jefferson Davis's grave is marked by a life-size statue.

GEORGE PICKETT

Confederate General
Born: January 16, 1825
Died: July 30, 1875

While many people have heard of Pickett's Charge, few know the details behind that disastrous attempt by the Confederates at Gettysburg.

George Pickett was a native son of Virginia. At age 17 he entered the U.S. Military Academy. Known as a prankster, he graduated last in his class. Soon thereafter he saw action in the Mexican-American War. In 1859 Pickett distinguished himself on San Juan Island when he was dispatched there to protect American farmers against British forces in what has become known as the Pig War.

Pickett resigned from the U.S. Army and joined the Confederate forces at the start of the Civil War. He soon reached the rank of brigadier general and saw much action. At the First Battle of Cold Harbor, Pickett was wounded seriously in the shoulder when he was shot off his horse. After his recovery Pickett was promoted to major general. Pickett's next major action was in July 1863 at Gettysburg. General Robert E. Lee wanted a large assault on Union lines at Cemetery Ridge. What followed is now known as Pickett's Charge, as several divisions of Confederate forces charged in an open field toward the Union army. This poorly thought-out attack resulted in more than 6,000 Confederate casualties compared to approximately 1,500 for Union forces. Upon

*George
Pickett's
Grave*

being told by Pickett himself that his division was gone, Robert E. Lee
decided to retreat and fight another day.

In April 1865 Pickett was involved in the Battle of Five Forks, another Confederate disaster. Pickett and other Confederate commanders had sneaked away for a relaxing shad bake (shad is a type of fish)
without informing subordinates of their exact location. While their
commanders were picnicking, Union forces attacked and devastated

the Confederate troops. This embarrassing defeat, coupled with the defeat of Lee's forces at Petersburg, contributed to Lee's surrender at Appomattox Courthouse on April 9, 1865.

Pickett died in 1875 at the age of 50 as the result of a liver abscess.

FUN FACT

Though Pickett's Charge bears his name, Pickett did not lead the assault. He was probably at a nearby farm, awaiting news of the battle's progress.

DIRECTIONS

At the main entrance follow Hollywood Avenue. At the intersection with Eastvale and Confederate Avenues, take a right onto Confederate. Follow Confederate Avenue past the Confederate Soldiers Monument. It will then loop in a circle. On the outer edge of the circle, close to Idlewood Avenue, you will find Pickett's elaborate marker.

J.E.B. STUART

Confederate General
Born: February 6, 1833
Died: May 12, 1864

James Ewell Brown Stuart, known as Jeb to his friends, was another proud native son of Virginia. Stuart was a good student who excelled at mathematics. He attended West Point and graduated in the upper tier of his class in 1854. Stuart was an excellent horseman and as a junior officer showed excellent leadership skills in the cavalry of the U.S. Army. His reconnaissance skills proved to be invaluable to his superiors.

Stuart was a bit of a dandy, wearing his trademark red-lined cape, gold sash, and plumed hat. He served in a variety of military campaigns, including conflicts with Native Americans, and in 1859 he volunteered as an aide to Colonel Robert E. Lee. He was there when Lee captured John Brown at Harpers Ferry. Before the start of the Civil War, Stuart was promoted to the rank of captain.

When Virginia seceded from the Union in 1861, Stuart quit the U.S. Army and joined the Confederate military. He was assigned to

J.E.B. Stuart's Grave

report to Thomas "Stonewall" Jackson, who quickly promoted Stuart to colonel. Stuart's daring exploits with his cavalry brigades at the
First Battle of Bull Run, in the Peninsula Campaign, and at Antietam drew the attention of the country and embarrassed Union forces.
He was soon promoted to the rank of major general. However, Stuart's
1863 misjudgment at the Battle of Gettysburg has haunted his military legacy. After receiving orders from General Lee to lead the cavalry
northward from Brandy Station, Virginia, to Gettysburg, Pennsylvania, Stuart took a circuitous route with the intention of surprising
Union troops along the way and inflicting as much damage as possible. However, Stuart and his men met heavy Union resistance, and it
is estimated that he arrived at Gettysburg two days later than if he had
taken a more direct route. The late arrival deprived General Lee of
Stuart's cavalry and his reconnaissance ability. Had Lee better information about Union positions and strength, the outcome of the Battle
of Gettysburg might have been different.

Stuart's military career came to an end the following year when, on May 11, 1864, he was fatally shot in the stomach at the Battle of Yellow Tavern. Stuart died the next day from his wound.

DIRECTIONS

From the main entrance take Hollywood Avenue. At the intersection with Eastvale and Confederate Avenues, take a right onto Confederate. Follow Confederate Avenue to the right past Cedar Avenue. Take the next left onto Western Avenue. Follow Western Avenue to Ellis Avenue, where you make a left. About 100 feet into the DE section, close to Ellis Avenue, you will find the Stuart monument.

CHAPTER SIX

West Point Cemetery

329 WASHINGTON ROAD

WEST POINT, NEW YORK 10996

W est Point Cemetery is located on the same grounds as the Military Academy in West Point, New York. Though it had been a cemetery, used by local residents, for a good many years prior to the opening of the Military Academy, it was designated a military cemetery in 1817. Close to and overlooking the Hudson River, it is a beautifully kept cemetery with impressive monuments. such as the obelisk-shaped Wood's Monument and the Cadet Monument with its detailed cannon sculpture. After Arlington Cemetery, it is arguably the second most popular military cemetery in the country.

An array of notable military names, from the American Revolutionary era to the present, can be found here. Only individuals who graduated from West Point, soldiers who died while assigned to West Point, and their family members are eligible for burial at this property of 12 acres. There are approximately 8,000 final resting places. Available plots for additional burials are limited, and it is expected that burial space will no longer be available within a few years. There are plans to expand the property for additional burials and cremated remains.

The cemetery is open seven days a week throughout the year, from sunrise to sunset. It is best to call the front office to get the exact hours for a particular day.

MARGARET CORBIN
Revolutionary War Heroine
Born: November 12, 1751
Died: January 16, 1800

Margaret Corbin is not buried at West Point Cemetery, though for a time it was believed that she was. What was intended as her gravestone now serves as a memorial to Corbin. So why are we including her in this book? We feel her contribution to the cause of American Independence warrants mention, as well as our gratitude.

Born in Pennsylvania as Margaret Cochran, she was married at age 21 to John Corbin, a farmer from Virginia. John Corbin was a patriot who joined the army to fight for the colonies' freedom from British rule. In November 1776 John Corbin was part of a garrison that remained behind as General George Washington retreated fol-

Margaret Corbin's Memorial

lowing an attack by British forces in the northern part of New York City. John Corbin operated a small cannon against the British Hessian forces. Margaret Corbin, as a nurse, was allowed to stay by her husband's side as he operated and fired his cannon. During the battle John Corbin was shot and killed, and Margaret took over the firing of the cannon. She continued to fire until she herself was severely wounded by gunfire.

She was taken prisoner by the British, but because of the severity of her wounds was soon released. Impressed by her bravery and sympathetic to her disabling injuries, the Continental Congress granted her one-half of a soldier's pay for the remainder of the war. Thus Corbin became the first woman in our history to receive a military pension.

Margaret Corbin died in 1800 at the age of 48.

FUN FACT

In 1926, it was believed, she was exhumed from her original burial site and reinterred in West Point Cemetery. However, in 2017 it was ascertained that the remains buried at West Point were not hers. The exact location of her true remains is unknown.

DIRECTIONS

Obtain a cemetery map from the cemetery office. The grave is located to the left of the Cadet Chapel in Section XI. This section is virtually devoid of gravestones, so her impressive large memorial stone stands out with its bronze relief.

EGBERT LUDOVICUS VIELE

Civil Engineer/Union General/Congressman
Born: June 17, 1825
Died: April 22, 1902

Okay, say it and get it out of your system. Who???!!! Feel better now? Good; let us proceed.

Born in New York State, Egbert Viele graduated from West Point in 1847 and entered the Army as a commissioned junior officer. He saw action in the Mexican-American War. In 1853 Viele left the Army to pursue a career in civil engineering. In 1855 he submitted a design proposal for Central Park in New York City. The proposal was not accepted, but Viele was appointed to be engineer in chief of Central Park.

Viele returned to Army service at the outset of the Civil War in 1860. He was commissioned a brigadier general and commanded Union forces in military campaigns in Georgia. He left the Army in 1863 and returned to civil engineering. In 1855 Viele developed a map of Manhattan's underground waterways that, incredibly, is still in use and is now appropriately called the Viele Map. In 1884 Viele was elected to a single term in the U.S. Congress.

Egbert Viele passed away in 1902.

FUN FACT

Viele and his wife are entombed in a tomb of his own design. It is in the shape of an Egyptian pyramid. Also within Viele's sarcophagus,

Egbert Viele's Tomb

per his instructions, a buzzer was installed just in case he were buried alive. It is our conjecture that this fear came from Viele's reading Edgar Allan Poe's "The Premature Burial" once too often.

DIRECTIONS

Viele's large Egyptian-style tomb is easy to spot since it stands out among the normal headstones in the cemetery. Located in Section XXXIV, facing the Cadet Chapel, it is almost directly behind the semicircle of columbaria in the middle of the cemetery.

GEORGE ARMSTRONG CUSTER

Legendary Army Commander
Born: December 5, 1839
Died: June 25, 1876

Most everyone has heard of Custer's Last Stand at Little Big Horn,
but few are aware of Custer's participation in a number of Civil War
battles.

George Armstrong Custer was born in Ohio. He entered West
Point in 1857 and graduated academically last in his class. A born
showoff and prankster, he was nearly expelled at West Point because
of a poor conduct record. Following graduation, he was commissioned
as a junior officer and participated in many Civil War battles, such as
the First Battle of Bull Run, Antietam, Gettysburg, and Appomattox
(where Lee surrendered to Grant). Custer was known for his gaudy

George Custer's Grave

dress, but more importantly he earned a reputation for bravery under enemy fire, and as a result became a hero for many schoolboys in the country. At the war's end Custer's rank was brevet brigadier general.

Custer remained in the army and was employed by General Philip Sheridan in various skirmishes and wars involving Native American tribes. In 1876 Custer met his end in Montana at the valley of the Little Bighorn in a campaign against Lakota Chief Sitting Bull, who had formed an alliance between the Sioux and the Cheyenne tribes. Despite being advised that the Indians had more than 2,000 warriors ready for battle, Custer decided to attack with his troop of only 647. Custer's strategy was to employ the element of surprise, so he divided his regiment to attack the Indian encampment from various sides. The result was catastrophic, with Custer and his troops wiped out. Custer was killed by bullet wounds to his head and near his heart.

FUN FACT

Ulysses Grant was not a particular admirer of Custer because of Custer's grandstanding and braggadocio.

DIRECTIONS

Custer's large obelisk is located in Section XXVII, which is northeast of the Cadet Chapel toward the back of the cemetery.

HERBERT NORMAN SCHWARZKOPF, JR.
Army Four-Star General
Born: August 22, 1934
Died: December 27, 2012

We both had the pleasure of meeting, on separate occasions, General Schwarzkopf. We concurred that he was an impressive man in person. One of us met him at a radio station when Schwarzkopf came in to promote his autobiography. The second met him at a book signing.

Herbert Norman Schwarzkopf, Jr., known as Norman, was born in New Jersey. Schwarzkopf's father, Herbert Norman Schwarzkopf, Sr., had a distinguished Army career before retiring as a major general in 1953. An outstanding student, the junior Schwarzkopf graduated from West Point in 1956.

Norman Schwarzkopf's Grave

Following graduation, he was commissioned with the rank of second lieutenant. In 1965 then Major Schwarzkopf saw his first tour of
duty in Vietnam. In combat he earned two Silver Star medals as well
as a Purple Heart. Schwarzkopf later returned to the United States for
a teaching assignment at West Point. In 1969, now a lieutenant colonel, Schwarzkopf began his second tour of Vietnam, where he earned
a third Silver Star and a second Purple Heart. In 1977 he was promoted
to brigadier general for his leadership in training troops at Fort Rich-

ardson in Alaska. In 1983, then a major general, Schwarzkopf was part of the command group that led the invasion of Grenada. In 1986 he was promoted to lieutenant general.

In 1988 Schwarzkopf, now a four-star general, was selected to head the U.S. Central Command. After Iraq invaded Kuwait in 1990, President George H. W. Bush, fearing that Iraq would next invade Saudi Arabia, took Schwarzkopf's advice for an overwhelming military strike to retake Kuwait. In January 1991 Operation Desert Storm commenced. As Schwarzkopf planned, the initial assault was a bombing campaign, and then ground troops were sent in and quickly decimated most of the Iraqi Republican Guard. On March 3, 1991, Schwarzkopf arrived in Kuwait City with the mission of retaking Kuwait from Iraq accomplished.

Shortly after the war, Norman Schwarzkopf retired from military service. Enormously popular with the American public, he was urged to run for public office. Schwarzkopf instead opted to write his autobiography, and he earned speaking fees for public appearances.

Norman Schwarzkopf died in 2012 from complications arising from pneumonia.

DIRECTIONS

Schwarzkopf's large headstone is in the front row of Section X, to the right of the Cadel Chapel, where the section begins opposite the columbarium.

ALONZO CUSHING
Civil War Hero of Gettysburg
Born: January 19, 1841
Died: July 3, 1863

A few years ago, when we learned of Alonzo Cushing's belated recognition for his bravery in the Civil War, we felt compelled to include him in this chapter.

Alonzo Cushing, born in Wisconsin, graduated from the United States Military Academy in 1861. After graduation he was commissioned as a first lieutenant. Cushing saw a great deal of action in a number of significant Civil War battles, including Antietam, Bull

Alonzo Cushing's Grave

Run, Fredericksburg, and Chancellorsville. Cushing lost his life heroically on the third and last day at Gettysburg.

At Gettysburg Cushing commanded a Union artillery battery at Cemetery Ridge, in defense against the Confederates' famed Pickett's Charge. Cushing was severely wounded by cannon shrapnel to his shoulder and stomach. Despite intense pain, he refused to give up his command post and continued to issue orders to his troops. Before the battle of Gettysburg concluded in Union victory, Cushing was killed by a bullet that entered his mouth and exited the back of his head. For his bravery he was posthumously promoted to brevet lieutenant colonel.

In 1987 a Wisconsin resident began a campaign to have Alonzo Cushing awarded the Congressional Medal of Honor. Finally, the medal was awarded in November 2014, 151 years after Cushing's death.

FUN FACT

Cushing's gravestone includes this appropriate tribute, at the behest of Cushing's mother: "Faithful unto Death."

DIRECTIONS

Cushing's small stone is located in Section XXVI, which is on the outer edge of the cemetery. Cushing lies adjacent to the large obelisk of General John Buford. In addition to the headstone, the grave has a flat brass marker.

CHAPTER SEVEN

Laurel Hill Cemetery

3822 RIDGE AVENUE

PHILADELPHIA, PENNSYLVANIA 19132

Laurel Hill Cemetery was founded in 1836 for reasons similar to those of other cemeteries described in this volume: the growing city of Philadelphia needed land for both commercial and residential purposes. Church graveyards were running out of room, and some concerned citizens decided it was time for the city to manage its burials more efficiently. Laurel Hill Cemetery became the second garden cemetery in the United States, after Mount Auburn Cemetery in Cambridge, Massachusetts.

The original 32 acres of property, now 81 acres, were chosen for their bucolic scenery and proximity to the Schuylkill River, which added to the serene atmosphere. The picturesque landscape and the vistas of the river and its curvy roads—along with the fact that Revolutionary War heroes were reinterred here—made this cemetery a popular site for family picnics, strolling, and carriage rides—so much so that, for a time, tickets were needed for admission.

Today, in addition to Revolutionary War notables, a number of Civil War generals as well as other historic persons are buried at Laurel Hill. This property earned the distinction of being designated a National Historic Landmark in 1998.

The hours are Monday–Friday from 8 a.m. to 4:00 p.m. and Saturday–Sunday from 9:30 a.m. to 4:30 p.m.

GEORGE MEADE

Union General
Born: December 31, 1815
Died: November 6, 1872

We love Civil War history, and we have been privileged to take a number of Civil War tours with our good friend and Civil War historian James McPherson. We've toured Gettysburg with Jim three times, each time seeing and learning something new. Our favorite Gettysburg site is the field where Pickett's Charge took place on the third and final day of that famous battle in 1863. The failure of Pickett's Charge to break through Union lines pushed General Robert E. Lee's Confederate Army of Northern Virginia into a forced retreat. The commanding Union general at Gettysburg, George Meade, and his army handed Lee a rare defeat. It is unfortunate that today George Meade

George Meade's Grave

is often overlooked. It is with appreciation that we include General Meade's gravesite here.

George Meade was born in Cádiz, Spain, where his father was serving as a naval agent for the U.S. government. Years later, after the Meade family returned to the United States, Meade enrolled at West Point and graduated in 1835. Meade's career in the Army was initially brief, as he resigned in 1836 to pursue a career as a civil engineer. When that didn't work out, he reenlisted in the army in 1842. Meade's bravery at the Battle of Monterrey during the Mexican–American War earned him a promotion to first lieutenant.

Following that war, Meade, still a member of the military, was involved in coastal surveying in New Jersey, Florida, and the Great Lakes. Shortly after the start of the Civil War in 1861, he was appointed brigadier general. Meade distinguished himself for bravery at many battlefronts, including the Second Battle of Bull Run, the Battle of South Mountain, Antietam, Fredericksburg, and Chancellorsville. During a series of battles near Richmond that have come to be known as the Seven Days Battles, Meade was severely wounded three times, shot in the arm, leg, and back.

When General Joseph Hooker resigned as the commander of the Army of the Potomac, President Lincoln appointed George Meade as his replacement. Just three days later, Meade confronted General Lee at the Battle of Gettysburg. Despite Meade's victory, President Lincoln was extremely disappointed that Meade did not pursue Lee into Virginia when the Confederate army retreated. Many felt that Meade's decision not to pursue Lee was a wasted opportunity to end the war right then and there.

When Ulysses Grant was appointed commanding general of all Union armies in 1864, Meade informed Grant that he would serve in any capacity; he even offered his resignation if Grant wished to take it. Grant refused Meade's resignation, and later that year he elevated Meade to the rank of major general.

After the war Meade held various military commands. In 1868, during Reconstruction, he became governor of the Third Military District, made up of the Southern states of Alabama, Georgia, and Florida. In 1865 Harvard bestowed on Meade an honorary doctorate of law.

Meade died on November 6, 1872, at the relatively young age of 56, from complications from pneumonia.

FUN FACT

It was discovered after President Lincoln's assassination that he had written a letter to General George Meade on July 14, 1863. In that letter Lincoln expressed his severe disappointment at Meade's decision not to follow Lee's army after the Battle of Gettysburg. The letter was unsigned and unsent. Some Lincoln aficionados speculate that Lincoln did not send the letter because he realized that, after three brutal days of intense battle, he too might have decided not to pursue Lee.

DIRECTIONS

From the main entrance on Ridge Avenue, walk about 100 feet straight past the Shrubbery section. Turn left for about 50 feet, and in the L Section you will see Meade's grave decorated with American flags.

JOHN PEMBERTON

Confederate General
Born: August 10, 1814
Died: July 13, 1881

When we discovered that Laurel Hill Cemetery contained not only the grave of the victor of the Battle of Gettysburg (George Meade), but also the final resting place of the defeated Confederate general of the Battle of Vicksburg, that was something we could not escape mentioning. Many people do not remember that Ulysses Grant captured the Mississippi city of Vicksburg the day after Meade defeated Lee at Gettysburg. Before those two battles, the war was generally going badly for the Union side. The dual, almost simultaneous victories at Gettysburg and Vicksburg thrilled the North, and the tide turned toward eventual Union victory.

John C. Pemberton was born in Philadelphia and graduated from West Point in 1833. Commissioned a second lieutenant, he saw action in the Seminole Indian War in 1837 and 1838. From 1846 to 1848 Pemberton was engaged in military campaigns in the Mexican–American War, seeing action in battles such as Monterrey and Vera Cruz. He was elevated to brevet captain as a result of this tour of duty.

John Pemberton's Grave

In 1848 Pemberton married Martha Thompson of Norfolk, Virginia. This marriage would later affect his allegiance in the Civil War. After various assignments at outposts in New Mexico, Minnesota, and Kansas, he found himself in garrison duty at the Washington Arsenal in the District of Columbia at the outbreak of the Civil War in 1861.

Despite protests from his family, the influence of his Virginia-born wife led Pemberton to resign his commission in the Union army. Initially commissioned a lieutenant colonel in the Confederate army, he rose to major general in January 1862. In October of that year, elevated to lieutenant general, he was assigned to defend the fortress city of Vicksburg. After a hard-fought battle lasting 11 days in June and July 1863, with the city surrounded by Grant's army, Pemberton was finally forced to capitulate.

Nearly 30,000 Confederate men surrendered at Vicksburg. Pemberton would remain a prisoner of war for more than three months, after which he was released in a prisoner exchange in October 1863. Pemberton then went seven months without an assignment. He resigned as a general officer in May 1864, but several days later he accepted President Jefferson Davis's offered commission as a lieutenant colonel of the artillery. Pemberton served at this lesser rank for the duration of the war.

At the conclusion of the Civil War, Pemberton lived on his farm near Warrenton, Virginia, from 1866 to 1876. He then returned to his home state of Pennsylvania, where he died in 1881. Despite vociferous protests, including from the family of General George Meade, the unrepentant Confederate officer was interred in Laurel Hill Cemetery. Meade and Pemberton are in different sections of the cemetery, but are within walking distance of each other.

DIRECTIONS

Enter the cemetery at the Ridge Avenue entrance. Upon entering you will find yourself on Hunting Park Avenue. Follow Hunting Park to its end, then make a left and walk about 50 feet. Turn right, looping around, until you see a red sign indicating Section 9. On the right of the sign is Pemberton's grave.

HELENA SCHAAFF SAUNDERS

Pianist/Composer
Born: May 24, 1823
Died: July 8, 1857

On our visit to Laurel Hill Cemetery, we came across an unusual monument and then learned of the touching story surrounding it. We were so moved that we decided to include it in our book.

Helena Schaaff Saunders, of German descent, was an accomplished pianist, music teacher, and composer of several Bavarian polkas. She met her husband, Henry Dmochowski Saunders, a renowned Polish sculptor, in a Philadelphia boarding house in the early 1850s after he came to the United States to escape the Russian occupation of Poland. They fell in love and married.

Helena Schaaff Saunders's Grave

Their first child died stillborn in 1855. Two years later, the second baby was delivered lifeless, and Helena too died as a result of childbirth. Devastated, Henry sculpted a tribute to his family. This haunting iconic sculpture, which took 18 months to complete, is known as the *Mother and Twins*. It sits in a prominent position in the cemetery overlooking the Schuylkill River.

After completing this tribute to his family in Laurel Hill, Henry returned to Poland, where he continued to sculpt. He also fought against the Russian occupation and died doing so in May 1863.

FUN FACT

Henry's sculptures of Thaddeus Kosciuszko and Casimir Pulaski are in the U.S. Capitol Building.

DIRECTIONS

From the main entrance on Ridge Avenue, walk straight back to the end of the cemetery facing the Schuylkill River. At the very edge on the left, the last monument you will see will be the Saunders memorial.

HENRY DERINGER

Inventor
Born: October 26, 1786
Died: February 28, 1868

As kids our favorite television show, hands down, was *The Wild Wild West* starring Robert Conrad and Ross Martin. This western takeoff on James Bond featured Secret Service agents James West and Artemus Gordon tackling villains with state-of-the-art technology (circa 1870, that is). One of our favorite devices used by agent James West was a derringer pistol, hidden up his sleeve, which could drop into his palm when necessary.

When we discovered that Henry Deringer, the inventor of the original Deringer pistol, was buried in Laurel Hill Cemetery, we definitely wanted to check out his gravesite. Because of their small size, Deringer's pistols became instantly popular. Men could conceal them in their pockets. These one-shot pistols became popular with women too, as some ladies liked to carry them in their purses for protection. It

John Wilkes Booth's Derringer

is unfortunate that John Wilkes Booth, who also appreciated the ease of concealing this weapon, used one to assassinate Abraham Lincoln.

Deringer was born in Easton, Pennsylvania, though his family moved to Philadelphia early in his childhood. His father, Henry Deringer, Sr., was a gunsmith who developed the Kentucky rifle, a widely used long-barreled hunting rifle.

After serving his apprenticeship with a Richmond gunsmith, Deringer moved back to Philadelphia in 1806. In 1825 he designed the first of what were later known as derringer pistols (note the lower case "d" and extra "r" in the spelling). As Henry Deringer never claimed a patent for his pistol's design, many copycat models flooded the market. Eventually Deringer pursued legal action to protect his brand against infringement, and the California Supreme Court ruling in *Deringer v. Plate* in 1865, granting him and his company protection, became a landmark in trademark law. In this case the court ruled that a trademark is a symbol associated with a commercial product, and thus imitators of the original Deringer pistol could not hide behind a slightly different spelling of the name to claim there was no infringement.

Nevertheless, competitor gunmakers found ways to evade the ruling, and by 1866 Remington Arms was manufacturing its own

Henry Deringer's Grave

"derringer" with a double barrel, a feature that further increased the popularity of these small pistols.

Deringer passed away in 1868 at the age of 81.

FUN FACT

Describing the Lincoln assassination, a reporter wrote that John Wilkes Booth used a "Derringer" pistol, misspelling the name with an extra "r." This mistake was widely repeated, particularly by copycat manufacturers, and thus the difference in spelling between the inventor and his creation.

DIRECTIONS

From the main entrance on Ridge Avenue, walk straight ahead, then slightly left into the circular area called the Shrubbery. Deringer's grave is about 50 feet ahead, on the right of the Shrubbery at the 3 o'clock position.

HARRY KALAS

Baseball Sportscaster
Born: March 26, 1936
Died: April 13, 2009

As non-Philadelphians, we were not familiar with Harry Kalas until his gravesite in Laurel Hill Cemetery grabbed our attention. It is so unique that we felt compelled to include him in this book.

For close to 40 years, Harry Kalas was an extremely popular sportscaster for the major league baseball team the Philadelphia Phillies. His flamboyant grave is situated on a scenic bluff above the Schuylkill River overlooking his beloved Philadelphia. Kalas's gravestone is eight feet tall, in the shape of a broadcast microphone, with the base shaped like home plate. The grave is surrounded by four actual baseball park seats taken from the old Veterans Stadium, where the Phillies used to play their games. The seats allow visitors to sit, pay their respects, and enjoy the view. And in a final nice touch, to make sure the spirit of Harry Kalas is at peace, his grave was resurfaced with sod that came from Citizens Bank Park, where the Phillies now play.

Harry Kalas's Grave

The inscribed base of Harry Kalas's Grave

Kalas was born in Chicago, graduated from the University of Iowa, and served his country in the United States Army. In 1961 Kalas began his sportscasting career, calling games for a minor league baseball team. In 1965 he made his major league debut as a broadcaster for the Houston Astros, and in 1971 Kalas made his way to the Philadelphia Phillies.

Highlights of his Philadelphia broadcast career included calling six no-hitters, six National League Championship series, and three World Series. Kalas's play-by-play style was easygoing, and he had a distinct baritone voice that rose when a play got exciting. His signature home run call of "Outta Here" became a part of his legend.

Kalas died of heart disease in 2009. He was on the job in the press box of Nationals Park, preparing to cover the Washington Nationals' season opener against the Phillies in 2009.

FUN FACT

Kalas became the fourth person in baseball history—after Babe Ruth, Jack Buck, and Miller Huggins—to lie in state in a major league park when his casket was displayed behind home plate at Citizens Bank Park.

DIRECTIONS

From the main entrance on Ridge Avenue, walk straight to the back of the cemetery. You will reach a ledge facing the Schuylkill River. At the foot of the ledge you will find Harry Kalas's microphone-shaped tombstone surrounded by seats from Veterans Stadium.

CHAPTER EIGHT

Kensico Cemetery

273 LAKEVIEW AVENUE EAST

VALHALLA, NEW YORK 10595

K ensico Cemetery is located in the hamlet of Valhalla, in the town-
ship of Mount Pleasant, within Westchester County in New York
State. Founded in 1889 because of a need for additional burial space,
this scenic property was developed to mirror nearby rural cemeteries such as Mount Auburn and Woodlawn. Well maintained, the 461
acres offer a tranquil setting for final resting places. The Sharon Gardens section of Kensico was established in the 1950s for Jewish burials.
Within Sharon Gardens can be found the final resting places of Academy Award–winning screenwriter Paddy Chayefsky and recent opera
greats Robert Merrill and Beverly Sills.

The cemetery is open every day of the year from 8:30 a.m. to 4:30
p.m. The cemetery office hours are 9 a.m. to 5 p.m. from Monday to
Friday, and 9 a.m. to 4 p.m. on Saturday. The office is closed on New
Year's Day, Thanksgiving, and Christmas.

HARRY FRAZEE

Baseball Owner/Theatrical Producer
Born: June 29, 1880
Died: June 4, 1929

As kids growing up in New York City, it was not difficult for us to
become baseball fanatics. The 1969 Miracle Mets, a team thought to
have little chance for success, shocked everyone and electrified New
York by winning the World Series in October 1969. The New York
Yankees were always colorful and fun to follow. Kensico Cemetery is one of our favorites because it has its share of baseball legends'
gravesites.

Harry Frazee was born in Illinois. He is notorious for being the
owner of the Boston Red Sox when the team sold Babe Ruth to the
New York Yankees in 1920. Growing up in Peoria, Frazee developed a
love for baseball, which he played with some skill. As a teenager Frazee
was also introduced to the world of the theater when he worked in
the Peoria Theater as an assistant manager. Frazee would eventually
become an actor, director, agent, and producer. After moving to Chicago, Frazee along with his financial partners had the Cort Theater
built in 1907. Frazee's production successes made him a millionaire.

He eventually moved to New York City, where he—again with financial partners—had Broadway's Longacre Theatre built.

Frazee bought the Boston Red Sox in 1917. The following season, the Red Sox won their fourth World Series in seven years. One of their stars was a young Babe Ruth, at the time an ace pitcher. Popular as Ruth was with the fans, his behavior off the field did not endear him to Red Sox management. Ruth had become known in Boston for his drunken antics, gambling, and carousing with prostitutes. All was forgiven as long as the team was winning and Ruth's pitching remained top notch. But the 1919 season was a major disappointment for the Red Sox. The insufferable Ruth wanted to quit pitching and demanded to play the outfield so that, as an everyday player, he would have more opportunities to demonstrate his home-run power. Red Sox management refused Ruth's request. With baseball attendance down, and mortgage payments on Fenway Park needing to be met, Frazee sold Ruth to the New York Yankees in a strictly cash deal for $100,000.

Frazee sold the Boston Red Sox in 1923. For the remainder of his life, he focused on theater productions; his biggest Broadway hit was the 1925 smash musical comedy *No, No, Nanette*.

Harry Frazee's Tomb (Courtesy of Joseph Connor)

Frazee died in 1929, just short of his 49th birthday, from kidney failure.

FUN FACT

The "Curse of the Bambino" was a legendary hex that diehard Red Sox fans blamed Frazee for. After the sale of Ruth to the Yankees in 1920, the Red Sox went 86 years before winning another World Series. During that time the team suffered through 26 New York Yankees World Series victories, in addition to a crushing, heart-breaking loss in the 1986 World Series to the New York Mets (no less!). When the Red Sox finally won the World Series again in 2004, the Curse of the Bambino was broken.

DIRECTIONS

Obtain both a section map and a tour map from the cemetery office. Frazee lies in Section 18, on Mohegan Avenue between Commerce Street and Tecumseh Avenue, after the Friars Club sign and up the hill.

JACOB RUPPERT

Baseball Owner/Businessman/Politician
Born: August 5, 1867
Died: January 13, 1939

Jacob Ruppert was born in New York City. Ruppert's father owned and operated a brewery. Though Ruppert had been accepted by Columbia University, he elected to join his father in the brewery instead, learning the business from the ground up. (As an aside, we both remember our father enjoying an occasional Ruppert's Knickerbocker Beer.) In 1898 Ruppert was elected to the House of Representatives, representing New York City's 15th congressional district in the Bronx, where he would serve for four terms. When Jacob Ruppert, Sr., died in 1915, the younger Ruppert inherited and became the president of his father's brewery.

Ruppert's love of baseball led him to purchase the New York Yankees with a partner in 1915. In 1919 Ruppert purchased Babe Ruth from Harry Frazee's Boston Red Sox. The historic Yankee sports dynasty was in the making, as Ruppert used purchases and trades to acquire

Jacob Ruppert's Mausoleum (Courtesy of Joseph Connor)

additional quality players such as Waite Hoyt, "Jumping" Joe Dugan, and Harvey Hendrick. In 1922, using personal funds, Ruppert began building the first Yankee Stadium, which was completed in 1923, and fittingly the Yankees won their first World Series that same year. Over the course of Ruppert's executive leadership, the Yankees won a total of seven World Series.

Ruppert died as a result of complications from phlebitis, an inflammation of the veins.

FUN FACT

Strangely, Jacob Ruppert's mausoleum lies just yards from the resting place of Harry Frazee, the man who sold Babe Ruth to him.

DIRECTIONS

Ruppert's mausoleum, number 19 on the tour map, is in Section 53, on the corner of Powhattan Avenue and Cherokee Avenue. It is up high, across from the Lehman mausoleum, behind the Cherokee Avenue/ Cherokee Plot sign.

SERGEI RACHMANINOFF

Pianist/Composer/Conductor
Born: April 1, 1873
Died: March 28, 1943

Sergei Rachmaninoff is considered by most classical music critics to be one of the greatest pianists of all time. Born in Russia into an aristocratic family of musicians, Rachmaninoff demonstrated his genius for playing the piano and composing music at a very young age. Influenced by Tchaikovsky and other Russian composers of the Romantic period, Rachmaninoff is noted for his creative approach in blending emotion, harmony, and the rhythmic use of high and low notes.

In 1892, at the age of 19, Rachmaninoff made his first public appearances. In his early performances, he introduced the critically acclaimed Prelude in C-sharp Minor and *Morceaux de fantaisie*, though his Symphony No. 1, which debuted in 1897, was poorly received. This criticism launched Rachmaninoff into a period of depression during which he was unable to compose anything for a few years. Rachmaninoff's depression was so severe that it took psychotherapy and hypnosis for him to regain his enthusiasm for composition.

In 1901 Rachmaninoff's Piano Concerto No. 2 was a triumph. In 1904 he became the conductor of the Bolshoi Theatre in Moscow, but political unrest in Russia led Rachmaninoff to move to Dresden, Germany, in 1906. While living in Dresden, he accepted an invitation to tour the United States. The subsequent tour included a stint conducting the Boston Symphony Orchestra, and as a result Rachmaninoff's popularity in America soared. In 1910 he returned to Russia, but was again driven out as a result of the Russian Revolution of 1917. In late 1918 he and his family settled in New York City, where Rachmaninoff signed a recording contract with the Victor Talking Machine Company (later RCA Records). Rachmaninoff's years in America witnessed extensive touring, but fewer new compositions. It was during these years that he composed his famous *Rhapsody on a Theme of Paganini*, which was later used in the ballet *Paganini*. The storyline of this ballet centers on a man who sells his soul to an evil spirit in exchange for perfection in art, and for a woman.

Rachmaninoff died in 1943 just a few days shy of his 70th birthday. The cause of death was advanced melanoma.

FUN FACT

Rachmaninoff's Piano Concerto No. 2 is prominently featured in the score for the 1945 British film *Brief Encounter*, which stars Trevor Howard and Celia Johnson. This underrated cinematic gem led us to our interest in Rachmaninoff.

DIRECTIONS

Rachmaninoff's gravesite is number 38 on the tour map, where Sections 188 and 187 come together at the intersection of Katonah Avenue and Pocantico Avenue. It is inside the circle.

Sergei Rachmaninoff's Grave

LOU GEHRIG
Baseball Legend
Born: June 19, 1903
Died: June 2, 1941

When we were growing up, we watched the 1942 movie classic *The Pride of the Yankees*, heaven knows how many times, so Lou Gehrig's grave was a must-find for us when we made our first visit to Kensico Cemetery. A native-born New Yorker, Lou Gehrig was arguably the greatest first baseman in baseball history. Fondly remembered as the "Iron Horse," Gehrig's played 2,130 consecutive games, a record that lasted for 56 years before Cal Ripken, Jr., of the Baltimore Orioles broke the record in 1995. Batting behind another baseball legend (Babe Ruth), Gehrig was an integral part of the Yankees' famed "Murderers' Row." With so many top-notch hitters in the lineup, Gehrig was given ample opportunity to drive in runs, which he often did. In 1927 Gehrig totaled 175 runs batted in, and he played 13 consecutive seasons in which he drove in more than 100 runs.

During the 1938 season, Gehrig complained of fatigue more often than he had ever before, and his season stats were his worst since he had joined the Yankees. At the start of the 1939 baseball season, his physical deterioration was pronounced. On April 30, 1939, Gehrig played in his 2,130th consecutive game, and on May 2 he voluntarily removed himself from the lineup and never played again. The next month, he was diagnosed with ALS.

Just two months after retiring from baseball, on July 4, 1939, Lou Gehrig was honored at Yankee Stadium with Lou Gehrig Appreciation Day. A capacity crowd that day heard Gehrig give his famous and emotional speech with the words, "Today I consider myself the luckiest man on the face of the earth."

Gehrig died just shy of his 38th birthday in 1941. His wake was held at Yankee Stadium, after which he was cremated.

FUN FACTS

1. Strangely, there is no complete video recording of Gehrig's Yankee Stadium farewell speech.

Lou Gehrig's Grave (Courtesy of Joseph Connor)

2. While the 1942 Gary Cooper film *The Pride of the Yankees* leads you to believe that the famous "luckiest man" line was the last in the speech, it was actually the second sentence.

DIRECTIONS

The site is No. 29 on the Tour map, in Section 80 on the section map. Take Cherokee Avenue to Ossipee Avenue. You will find the site on the circle, before Lakeside Drive, behind the Ossipee Avenue/Cherokee Plot sign. Gehrig lies between and behind the Winkhaus headstone and the Penny headstone.

AYN RAND
Philosopher/Writer
Born: February 2, 1905
Died: March 6, 1982

Curious, provocative, outlandish, perplexing, and contradictory are adjectives that can be applied to Ayn Rand and her philosophy, which she called objectivism. Objectivism places a strong emphasis on individualism, arguing that human happiness is based on self-interest and not altruism. The virtues that people should develop, according to Rand, were reason, self-responsibility, integrity, pride, and productivity.

Having studied Rand at various points during our respective college careers, we concur that the tenets of her philosophy have influenced the current political climate in the United States. On the side of the people, we see Rand's influence in the increased interest in libertarian resistance to government requirements; on the side of the government, we see it in allowing individuals to opt out of governmental mandates or services. Contemporary admirers of Rand include former Federal Reserve Chairman Alan Greenspan, Supreme Court Justice Clarence Thomas, and former House Speaker Paul Ryan. Whether the tenets of objectivism and the rise of Donald Trump have any parallels, we will leave for the political pundits to argue about.

Born as Alisa Zinovyevna Rosenbaum in Russia, Rand saw the ill effects that the Russian Revolution of 1917 had on her family. During her university years she majored in history and studied philosophical writings. She was greatly influenced by the Greek philosopher Aristotle.

Rand came to the United States in 1925 and four years later married aspiring actor Frank O'Connor. Rand earned her living writing screenplays and novels. In 1933 she wrote a play titled *Night of January 16th*, a courtroom drama that was produced on Broadway. In her writings, including her two most famous novels, *The Fountainhead* and *Atlas Shrugged*, her main characters typically embodied the principles of objectivist philosophy. This can clearly be seen in *The Fountainhead*'s protagonist, Howard Roark, a bold and highly innovative architect. Roark is uncompromising in his architectural designs and would rather walk away from a lucrative project than submit to changes he

Ayn Rand's Grave (Courtesy of Joseph Connor)

does not agree with. The character of Roark trusts himself (self-inter-est) and his own ideas (integrity) and in doing so remains productive. By not bending to the judgment of others, Roark maintains the virtue of reason, achieves happiness, and benefits society as a whole.

Ayn Rand died in 1982 as the result of heart failure.

FUN FACTS

1. Ayn Rand supported Barry Goldwater for president in 1964, but could not abide Ronald Reagan in 1980. Rand's disdain for Reagan stemmed from Reagan's close association with the religious right. Rand, an atheist, thought religion hindered people from

assuming their true nature and pursuing self-interest. In addition, on the issue of abortion Reagan was pro-life, while Rand was pro-choice. Barry Goldwater, it may surprise some people to learn, was pro-choice and later in his career publicly expressed his own disdain for the religious right.

2. Rand's novel *Atlas Shrugged* ranks among the most widely read novels in world history. Sales for this book sharply increased following the financial meltdown of 2008.

DIRECTIONS

The grave is number 17 on the tour map. It is in Section 41 at the intersection of Cherokee Avenue and Ossipee Avenue.

ANNE BANCROFT

Actress
Born: September 17, 1931
Died: June 6, 2005

Anne Bancroft was a multitalented performer. She was an actress, director, screenwriter, and singer. An excellent actress, she was adept at both dramatic and comedic roles on stage and on screen. She is probably best known for her performance as the seductress Mrs. Robinson starring opposite Dustin Hoffman in *The Graduate*. For us, Anne Bancroft made a particular impression in her Academy Award–winning performance as Anne Sullivan in *The Miracle Worker*.

Born in the Bronx to blue-collar parents as Anna Maria Louisa Italiano, she studied at the Actors Studio under Lee Strasberg. Her first forays into acting were on early live television dramas. Anne Bancroft made her film debut opposite Marilyn Monroe in *Don't Bother to Knock* in 1952.

In 1958, making her Broadway debut opposite Henry Fonda in *Two for the Seesaw*, Bancroft won her first Tony Award. Her second Tony Award quickly followed in 1960 for her portrayal as the teacher Anne Sullivan opposite Patty Duke as Helen Keller in *The Miracle Worker*. Both actresses reprised their roles on screen in 1962 and won Academy Awards.

Anne Bancroft's Grave (Courtesy of Joseph Connor)

In 1964 Bancroft married comedic director/writer Mel Brooks. Her role in 1964's *The Pumpkin Eater* earned Bancroft's a second Academy Award nomination. This was followed by a number of movie appearances that included *The Graduate*, *The Turning Point*, and *To Be or Not to Be*. She made her screenwriting and directorial debut in 1980

with the comedy *Fatso*. Bancroft won an Emmy Award for her singing and acting in the CBS special *Annie, the Women in the Life of a Man*
in 1970.

In the 1990s and early 2000s she took on many supporting roles
on both screen and television, in productions such as *Honeymoon in
Vegas, Malice, Point of No Return, Home for the Holidays, Great Expectations,
Heartbreakers*, and *The Roman Spring of Mrs. Stone*. Her final appearance
was in 2004 in HBO's *Curb Your Enthusiasm*, in which she portrayed
herself.

Anne Bancroft died in 2005 as the result of uterine cancer. Her
husband, Mel Brooks, never left her side as she faced her end in the
hospital. This underscored their intense love for each other.

FUN FACTS

1. In the film *The Graduate*, in which Bancroft played the "older
   woman" opposite Dustin Hoffman, she was in actuality only six
   years older than he.
2. Anne Bancroft is one of only nine actors/actresses to have won
   both an Academy Award and a Tony Award for the same role.
3. Bancroft's tombstone is unusual and poignant. On top of the
   tombstone is a weeping angel.

DIRECTIONS

The grave is in Section 180 at the corner of Seneca Avenue and Pocantico Avenue, behind a tree.

CHAPTER NINE

Non–Cemetery Graves

I n this chapter we will cover some of our favorite resting places that are not contained in a typical cemetery or memorial park.

Mount Vernon

3200 MOUNT VERNON MEMORIAL PARK
MOUNT VERNON, VIRGINIA 22121

Many historical places claim that George Washington slept there, but at Mount Vernon we know with 100% certainty that, yes, Washington did actually sleep there. The Washington family had owned the land since the 1670s. Washington's half-brother Lawrence had inherited the property, and when Lawrence passed away he left half of the property to George, whom he had permitted to live on the grounds. The other half belonged to Lawrence's widow. Construction of the present house began in 1758. When Lawrence's widow passed away in 1761, George became the sole owner of Mount Vernon. Mount Vernon was designated a National Historic Landmark in 1960.

Mount Vernon

On the property today, one can visit the house where George and Martha Washington resided. Public access is permitted for the gardens and the grounds as well. One can also view Washington's two tombs: the original tomb, where Washington was first buried in 1799, and the second one, to which his remains and those of Martha were transferred in 1837. A more secure resting place was needed for Washington's remains after a failed attempt to steal his skull by a disgruntled former employee of Mount Vernon.

Mount Vernon is owned and maintained in trust by the Mount Vernon Ladies' Association. A museum on the property affords visitors the opportunity to view many artifacts that were owned by George and Martha.

The hours are typically 9 a.m. to 5 p.m. every day of the year. Tickets must be purchased to gain entrance to the property. A discount may be available if the tickets are purchased online.

GEORGE WASHINGTON
U.S. President
Born: February 22, 1732
Died: December 14, 1799

We have had the pleasure of visiting Mount Vernon, the home of George Washington, arguably America's most famous citizen, a number of times. As Mount Vernon receives no government funding, one of us is in the habit of making several tax-deductible★ donations each year for the preservation of Washington's residence and surrounding property. Only about 15 miles from Washington, DC, the grounds at Mount Vernon are impeccable, the house is magnificent, the visitor's center is splendid, and the museum is wonderful. We always find it a moving experience when we get to Washington's tomb and realize we are just a few yards away from the remains of the man who has been referred to as "first in the hearts of his countrymen." America

★It should be noted that we have nothing to do with fundraising, nor are we affiliated with Mount Vernon. We just feel strongly that Washington's legacy should never be taken for granted. We hope more people feel the same way after visiting Mount Vernon.

had a number of Founders, and certainly George Washington couldn't have done it by himself. But if George Washington had not existed, it would be safe to say that America, as we know it now, would never have existed.

Born into a wealthy family of tobacco planters in Virginia, Washington was trained in mathematics, trigonometry, and surveying. However, his ambition was to join the military, which he did in 1752 when he joined the Virginia militia. Two years later he participated in the French and Indian War. Washington quickly distinguished himself as a young officer, demonstrating courage and leadership skills under fire.

By the 1770s Washington grew impatient with Great Britain's rule over the colonies, particularly over the issue of taxation without representation. After the war for independence began with the battles of Concord and Lexington in April 1775, the Second Continental Congress named Washington commander in chief of the Continental Army. Washington, like many others, was willing to sacrifice everything in what we call today the Revolutionary War.

Historians typically do not consider George Washington a brilliant general with regard to strategies and tactics. Yes, Washington won important battles during the war, but he lost a good many also. However, despite his defeats, Washington was never captured, and he survived to fight another day. Those who fought with him noted his courage and the way he led by example, which inspired his men in battle. He was tough but fair, he never hogged credit, he treated everyone in a respectful manner, and as a result many of his officers were extremely loyal to him.

After Cornwallis's surrender in 1781 at Yorktown, major fighting stopped, and in 1783 the Treaty of Paris was signed, with the British recognizing America's independence.

Washington, a delegate from Virginia, was chosen as president of the Constitutional Convention at Philadelphia in 1787. After the Convention established our U.S. Constitution, he was unanimously elected by the Electoral College to be president of the United States. On April 30, 1789, Washington took his first oath of office in downtown New York City.

The young republic faced many challenges, which Washington met with strong leadership. He established the cabinet system, avoided conflict with Great Britain, did not get involved in the French revolution, suppressed the Whiskey Rebellion (initially leading the army that quelled it), and supported Alexander Hamilton's programs to settle all federal and state debts. Washington put the young nation on the secure road to becoming the power it is today. In 1793 the Electoral College chose him for a second term, again unanimously, and he is the only president to receive this honor.

After his second term, he retired to Mount Vernon, where he oversaw his plantation and received many guests. On December 12, 1799, he spent several hours in rain, hail, and snow surveying his property. Upon returning the next day, he awoke with a severe sore throat but still went out in the heavy snow to mark trees on the plantation. The next day he had great difficulty breathing and swallowing. The doctors who attended him believed in bloodletting as a cure and did so with him. This further debilitated him and led to his death on December 14. His last words were "'Tis well."

FUN FACTS

1. Contrary to what is commonly believed, George Washington did not have wooden false teeth. In fact, he had several sets made of ivory as well as animal and human teeth, the latter coming mostly from slaves. They can be seen today at the museum on the grounds of Mount Vernon.
2. Washington had a fear of being buried alive, and the funeral was held four days after his death to ensure this didn't happen.

MARTHA WASHINGTON
America's First "First Lady"
Born: June 2, 1731
Died: May 22, 1802

Martha Dandridge was born on her parents' plantation in Virginia. At the age of 18 in 1750, she married a wealthy planter, Daniel Park Custis, who was two decades her senior. They had four children together, and upon his death in 1757 she became an extremely wealthy widow, with over 17,500 acres of land and more than 300 slaves. She was an astute manager of the plantation.

On January 6, 1759, Martha Custis married George Washington, uniting two wealthy estates. They did not have any children together. It is believed that Washington was infertile, most likely from being exposed to his older brother's tuberculosis.

Content to live on the Mount Vernon property, Martha supported her husband during the Revolutionary War. She followed him to the winter encampments every year that the war was fought. Martha did her best to keep up the morale of the officers' wives.

Martha was not happy with, and did not support, Washington's decision to assume the presidency of the new nation. In fact, she did not attend his inauguration in New York on April 30, 1789. Ultimately she made the decision to support her husband, and she hosted many receptions for him during his presidency.

After the couple retired to Mount Vernon in 1797, Martha survived George by only two and a half years. Upon her death in 1802, as stipulated in George Washington's will, all of their slaves were freed.

George and Martha Washington's Tomb

United First Parish Church

1306 HANCOCK STREET
QUINCY, MASSACHUSETTS 02169

United First Parish Church, a Unitarian Universalist church in Quincy, Massachusetts, was established in 1639. The church has a Greek temple front supported by four monolithic columns. It was constructed in 1828, two years after President John Adams's death, and financed by the Adams family. Most of the granite used in the construction came from Adams family property. Interestingly, the original church tower bell was cast by Paul Revere.

As both John Adams and his son John Quincy Adams worshipped at this church, it is sometimes called the Church of the Presidents. Both presidents, as well as their wives, Abigail and Louisa, are entombed in a family crypt in the basement of the church.

United First Parish Church (Courtesy of John and Melissa Capuano)

Tours of the church and the tomb are offered on a walk-in basis and are typically available from mid-April to mid-November. The tour hours are Monday–Saturday, 11 a.m. to 4 p.m., and Sunday, 12 p.m. to 4 p.m.

JOHN ADAMS
U.S. President
Born: October 30, 1735
Died: July 4, 1826

As American history buffs, we naturally have a keen interest in our presidents, both their personal lives and their administrations. Some presidents, in our opinion, are overrated, and others are underappreciated. We believe that John Adams falls into the latter category.

John Adams was born in Braintree (now Quincy), Massachusetts. An exceptional student, he graduated from Harvard at the age of 20. After a brief stint as a teacher, Adams pursued a career as a lawyer.

Adams married Abigail Smith in 1764, and this led to a long and primarily happy marriage. They shared common interests and seemingly became of one mind, with Abigail serving as her husband's most trusted advisor.

Despite his opposition to British methods of tax collection, such as the Stamp Act of 1765, Adams demonstrated his scrupulous honesty by agreeing to defend British soldiers involved in what we call today the Boston Massacre. Adams believed everyone was entitled to a fair trial and counsel, and he won acquittal for six British soldiers accused of firing their rifles into a crowd of people.

Adams's opposition to British rule came to a head in 1774 when he became a member of the Continental Congress. He pushed vigorously for American independence, and it was Adams who asked Thomas Jefferson to write a Declaration of Independence in 1776.

In the following year he was named commissioner to France, and in 1779 he was appointed as the sole minister charged with negotiating peace with England. In 1783 Adams was instrumental in constructing the Treaty of Paris, which in essence ended the Revolutionary War. In 1785 he was appointed as the new nation's first minister to the Court of St. James—that is, ambassador to Great Britain.

*John Adams's
Tomb*
(Courtesy of
John and Melissa
Capuano)

In America's first presidential election in 1789, John Adams was elected vice president. The mostly ceremonial position frustrated Adams, but in presiding over the Senate he cast a tie-breaking vote 31 times, all in support of the Washington administration. This is the most tie breakers of all vice presidents.

In 1796 Adams was elected to the presidency with Thomas Jefferson as the new vice president. His dogmatic, never-yielding, "my way or the highway" style earned him many political foes, as well as criticisms from his own political base. He signed the controversial Alien and Sedition Acts, which stifled free speech, and most historians consider this his biggest mistake. However, when conflict erupted with France, Adams averted war and signed a peace treaty in 1800. Adams built up the U.S. Army and Navy and is known as the Father of the American Navy.

After losing the election of 1800 to Jefferson, Adams was so bitter with his former good friend that he left in the predawn hours of March 4 and did not attend his successor's inauguration. After not speaking for 12 years, they reconciled and started a lengthy correspondence. Adams lost his beloved wife Abigail in 1818. In 1824 he was thrilled when his son John Quincy was elected president. Befitting his legacy, he died on the 50th anniversary of the Declaration of Independence, July 4, 1826. Unaware that Jefferson had died earlier in the day, he uttered the last words, "Jefferson still survives." Having lived 90 years and 247 days, Adams was our longest living former president until he was surpassed in the 21st century by Ronald Reagan, Gerald Ford, George H. W. Bush, and Jimmy Carter.

FUN FACTS

1. Benjamin Franklin characterized Adams as "always an honest man, often a wise one, but sometimes, and in some things, absolutely out of his senses."
2. Adams gave Jefferson four reasons for not wanting to write the Declaration of Independence himself: "I am obnoxious, suspected, and unpopular. And you can write ten times better than I can."

ABIGAIL ADAMS

U.S. First Lady
Born: November 22, 1744
Died: October 28, 1818

Renowned historian Joseph Ellis calls Abigail Adams one of the most extraordinary women in American history, and in our opinion she lives up to that characterization.

Born Abigail Smith in Massachusetts, she received little formal schooling because of health problems. She was schooled at home, however, and she loved to read. Even at a young age, she surprised many by her knowledge of many subjects, particularly issues of the day.

She first met John when she was fifteen years old, and despite reservations from her mother, they were married when she was 20 years

Abigail Adams's Tomb
(Courtesy of John and Melissa Capuano)

of age. She brought up her five children (a sixth was stillborn), instilling in them the value of virtue. The family moved to Boston in 1768, and in 1774 to a farm in Braintree.

Like her husband, Adams strongly favored American independence. John always sought Abigail's advice regarding the war. She was so influential that some consider her a sort of founding mother. After the war, Abigail joined her diplomat husband in Paris in 1784. The following year she went to London as the wife of the ambassador. In 1788 the family returned home to Quincy.

In 1797, when John Adams became the nation's second president, Abigail—unlike her predecessor, Martha Washington—took an active role in her husband's administration. She hosted a formal dinner each week and made frequent public appearances. John Adams's political foes would refer to her sarcastically as "Mrs. President." Abigail was an early advocate of women's rights, arguing for married women to have property rights and supporting more opportunities for women, particularly in the field of education. Her advice to women was to educate themselves and not be so subservient to men. Abigail believed that all men, were they given the opportunity, would be tyrants.

In 1801, after her husband left the presidency, they returned to Quincy. Abigail died of typhoid fever in 1818. Her last words were, "Do not grieve, my friend, my dearest friend. I am ready to go. And

John, it will not be long." She is entombed by her husband's side in the Adams family crypt.

FUN FACT

Abigail chided John for his long absences from home. During one particularly long absence, she wrote him, "No man who is sixty should live more than three months from his family." John, a bit irked, replied, "How dare you hint or lisp a word about sixty years of age. If I were near I would soon convince you that I am not above forty!"

JOHN QUINCY ADAMS

U.S. President
Born: July 11, 1767
Died: February 23, 1848

As we mentioned earlier, we believe that the senior Adams's presidency is underappreciated. Most historians do not rate the John Quincy Adams presidency very highly either. John Quincy at best is ranked as a mediocre president. We tend to agree with that assessment. However, John Quincy Adams was still a great man! We will explain.

Born to John and Abigail Adams in Braintree, Massachusetts, John Quincy was a "chip off the old block." As a young man he exhibited high intelligence and was very well read. John Quincy often accompanied his father when the senior Adams traveled overseas on diplomatic missions. He learned and spoke several languages fluently. John Quincy graduated from Harvard in 1787. He then went on to study law, and he became a lawyer in 1790.

George Washington thought so highly of John Quincy Adams that he named him minister to the Netherlands and later to Portugal. At Washington's urging, his father, the second president, named him minister to Prussia. In between these diplomatic posts, he met and married Louisa Catherine Johnson, the daughter of the U.S. consul general in London.

In 1802 John Quincy was elected to the Massachusetts state house. He was elected to the U.S. Senate in 1803 and served until 1808. In 1809 the newly elected President James Madison tapped Adams to become minister to Russia. Adams was recalled from Russia to serve as the chief negotiator for the Treaty of Ghent that ended the War of 1812 with Great Britain. In addition, President Madison later appointed him Minister to the Court of St. James.

In April 1817 newly elected President James Monroe made Adams his secretary of state. In that position Adams successfully negotiated the Adams-Onis Treaty with Spain in 1821, transferring Florida to the United States and establishing the Sabine River as the boundary of the Louisiana Territory. Still, President Monroe was very concerned about foreign interference with the newly independent countries of Latin America. Former presidents Thomas Jefferson and James Madison urged Monroe to seek an alliance with Great Britain for the defense of the Western hemisphere. However, Monroe instead followed the advice of his secretary of state that any foreign attempt to establish a foothold in the Americas should be viewed as a hostile act. This became the Monroe Doctrine, which was issued in December 1823. Many historians have expressed the opinion that it should be called the Adams Doctrine and that John Quincy Adams should be acknowledged as one of America's greatest secretaries of state.

Initially the presidential election of 1824 produced no apparent winner. When the Electoral College completed voting, no candidate had reached the required majority. The Constitution states that in such an event, it is the responsibility of the House of Representatives to choose the next president. Andrew Jackson had received a plurality of the electoral votes, with John Quincy Adams coming in second and Henry Clay third. Before the balloting in the House, Adams met with Clay, and Clay agreed to release his electors to Adams, thereby giving him the votes needed to win. Jackson cried unfair when Adams named Henry Clay his secretary of state, insinuating that a sleazy quid pro quo deal had been made between Adams and Clay.

As president John Quincy Adams sought to modernize the American economy and promote education. Adams proposed that an income tax be collected for infrastructure purposes, such as improving the country's roads. Adams's agenda was often thwarted by his opponents in the Congress, who were loyal Jackson supporters. John Quincy Adams also did himself no favors, since his stiff and cool manner did not endear him even to his own supporters.

In the election of 1828 Andrew Jackson portrayed Adams as an out-of-touch elitist. Jackson, who characterized himself as the champion of the people, won the election handily. Emulating his father, John Quincy did not attend the inauguration of Jackson.

Bored in retirement, Adams decided to return to the political arena. He ran for and won a seat in the House of Representatives in 1830. He ended up being elected to nine terms and serving 17 years until his death in 1848.

During his tenure in the House he became the most prominent national leader opposing slavery. Notable was his defense of African slaves who had revolted and seized the Spanish ship *Amistad*. Adams argued their case before the U.S. Supreme Court and secured their acquittal, setting them free to return to their homes. Adams was often very articulate during the House floor debates. This earned him the nickname "old man eloquent."

In 1848 Adams was fatally stricken with a cerebral hemorrhage at his desk in the House. He lingered two days in the Speaker's room,

The Tombs of John Quincy Adams and Louisa Adams
(Courtesy of John and Melissa Capuano)

dying with his wife by his side. His last words were "This is the last of earth. I am content."

FUN FACTS

1. John Quincy Adams, when he was president, enjoyed early morning skinny-dipping in the Potomac River. One morning Anne Royall, a reporter, followed him, and after he dived into the river she called out to him. She sat on his clothes and refused to give them to him until he consented to an interview. Adams acquiesced, got his clothes back, and gave her the interview.
2. John Quincy Adams was the first president to have married a woman born outside the United States. This did not happen again until Donald Trump assumed office in 2017 with his wife Melania.

LOUISA ADAMS
U.S. First Lady
Born: February 12, 1775
Died: May 15, 1852

Louisa Catherine Johnson was born in London to an American merchant, Joshua Johnson. In 1790 Joshua Johnson was appointed U.S. Consul General, and John Quincy Adams met Louisa in 1795 when he visited Mr. Johnson. The couple married in 1797 in London.

Louisa was often sickly and had several miscarriages during her marriage. She did eventually bear four children. Having grown up in London and France, she found Massachusetts dull and uninteresting. She did, however, develop a deep affection for her in-laws, whom she came to love and respect.

When Adams was appointed minister to Russia, Louisa went with him. She survived Russian cold winters, strange customs, limited funds, and her often poor health. Despite these hardships she became a favorite of the czar, making up for her husband's lack of charm.

When peace negotiations for the Treaty of Ghent called Adams to London, she joined him, braving a 40-day journey across war-ravaged Europe by coach.

When Louisa's husband was named secretary of state in 1817, the family moved to Washington, DC, where Louisa's drawing room became a center for the diplomatic corps. Tuesday evenings were designated for music, and Louisa would play the harp, with which she was very proficient.

After moving into the White House in 1825, Louisa was taken aback by the hostility that her husband encountered, and she suffered bouts of depression. Yet she continued to entertain. Her cordial hospitality was evident to all who attended her weekly "drawing rooms."

Louisa looked forward to retirement in Massachusetts. However, that hope was dashed when her husband returned to Washington after being elected to the House of Representatives. Louisa survived her husband by four years, dying of a heart attack in 1852. It is a tribute to her that the enmity encountered by her husband in the White House did not extend to her. The day of her funeral marked the first time that both houses of Congress adjourned for a period of mourning for a woman.

The General Grant National Memorial
(GRANT'S TOMB)
RIVERSIDE DRIVE AND 122ND STREET
NEW YORK, NEW YORK 10027

The General Grant National Memorial is the largest mausoleum in North America. It houses the remains of General Ulysses S. Grant and his wife Julia in two side-by-side red granite sarcophagi modeled after Napoleon's sarcophagus at Les Invalides in Paris.

When Ulysses Grant died in 1885, the mayor of New York City, William Russell Grace, proposed to the Grant family that Grant be buried in New York. The family agreed, and the mayor then sought both public and private funds to build a proper monument. After planning and fundraising, construction began in 1891 and was completed in 1897, allowing Grant's remains to be transferred from a temporary resting place in Riverside Park.

The mausoleum is under the management of the National Park Service. There are exhibit galleries within the tomb as well as a Visitors Center. Admission is free. The memorial is open Wednesday through

The General Grant National Memorial

Sunday, 10 a.m. to 11 a.m., noon to 1 p.m., 2 p.m. to 3 p.m., and 4 p.m. to 5 p.m. The memorial is closed on Thanksgiving and Christmas.

ULYSSES S. GRANT

U.S. President
Born: April 27, 1822
Died: July 23, 1885

Our parents, one summer day when we were very young took us to Grant's Tomb. This may have been the first grave we ever visited. Anyone who has gotten this far in the book knows by now that we are Civil War buffs, and perhaps that day was the start of our fascination.

Considered one of the top military commanders in U.S. history, Ulysses S. Grant was born in Point Pleasant, Ohio. Shy and reserved as a boy, Grant was an average student who demonstrated great skill in horsemanship. Grant graduated from West Point in 1843 and served under General Winfield Scott during the Mexican-American War. He married Julia Dent in 1848. In 1854, then Captain Grant, facing allegations of drunken behavior, resigned from the Army. Grant then struggled financially, working on his brother-in-law's farm and in his father's tannery business. At one point the despondent Grant, wearing his faded Army jacket, was forced to sell firewood on the streets of St. Louis. This was an arduous time for Grant.

At the outbreak of the Civil War, Grant re-enlisted in the Army with the rank of major. His success story is the stuff legends are made of. He quickly rose through the ranks and, after being appointed major general, defeated Confederate Lieutenant General John C. Pemberton (see the chapter on Laurel Hill Cemetery) in the Battle of Vicksburg, often considered a turning point of the war. His strategic genius and thirst for victory earned him the nickname "Unconditional Surrender" Grant. Abraham Lincoln promoted him to lieutenant general and commanding general of the Army in March 1864. The surrender of Robert E. Lee at Appomattox in April 1865 effectively ended the Civil War.

When the war ended, Grant clashed repeatedly with Lincoln's successor, Andrew Johnson, about continuing Lincoln's policy of Reconstruction in the South. Elected president in his own right in 1868, Grant oversaw the passage of the 15th Amendment giving African Americans the right to vote. He strongly advocated the federal enforcement of civil rights, and his attorney general, Amos Akerman, vigorously prosecuted the Ku Klux Klan. Despite two financial scandals in which he was not implicated, his tenure as president is now regarded as being progressive and moving the country forward after the debacle of the Civil War.

After the conclusion of his presidency, Grant toured the world for two years and then settled in Manhattan in a townhouse on East 66th Street. He became a partner in the firm Grant and Ward, a brokerage house on Wall Street. His naïveté caught up with him when his part-

Ulysses and Julia Grant's Tomb

ner, Ferdinand Ward, defrauded him of his entire fortune. In an epic and courageous struggle, while battling deadly and painful cancer of the tongue and throat, Grant penned his memoirs so that his family would not be destitute. He completed the manuscript just days before he died in 1885 at a cottage on Mount McGregor in Saratoga County, New York. Immediately after the work's publication, his widow Julia began receiving royalty checks that eventually totaled $500,000, providing the financial means for the family to survive.

FUN FACTS

1. The publisher of Grant's memoirs was none other than Mark Twain. His affection for Grant is evidenced by the fact that he gave Grant the unheard-of royalty of 75% of all net sales.

2. Grant to this day maintains the reputation of being a heavy drinker. As it turns out, Grant really could not hold his liquor well. One or two drinks and Grant would become drunk.

Worth Square

5TH AVENUE, BROADWAY, AND 25TH STREET
NEW YORK, NEW YORK 10010

Worth Square is located at the intersection of Broadway and Fifth Avenue at 25th Street near midtown Manhattan, New York City. William Jenkins Worth was a celebrated general at the time of his death, and New York City leaders quickly agreed to erect an elaborate monument in his memory. The monument, just above Worth's final resting place, is a handsome 51-foot-high obelisk made of Quincy granite, surrounded by an ornamental cast-iron fence. Central decorative bands are inscribed with the names of battle sites significant to Worth's

General William Jenkins Worth Monument

career. On the front is a bronze equestrian relief of Worth, and on the back is a bronze dedicatory plaque.

Having lived in New York City all our lives, we must have passed by the Worth Monument more times than we can count. However, it wasn't until a few years ago that we uncovered the fact that it wasn't just a monument, but also a grave. We discovered this fact on a website about unusual gravesites in and around New York City.

WILLIAM JENKINS WORTH
Army General
Born: March 1, 1794
Died: May 7, 1849

Born in Hudson, New York, to Quaker parents, William Worth initially went to work in the mercantile field. However, when the War of 1812 began, Worth joined the Army and began a distinguished military career. Commissioned as a lieutenant in 1813, he served as an aide to Brigadier General Winfield Scott. In the Battle of Lundy's Lane, he was severely wounded in the thigh by canon grapeshot and barely survived. Despite the ensuing disability, Worth remained in the military and was promoted to brevet major. He then served as commandant of the cadets at West Point, where he established the importance of discipline in military training. Also at West Point he established the policy of promotion based on a cadet's merit: no longer would favoritism be shown a cadet because of his family name. Worth's words about the virtue of impartiality for an officer are still part of West Point's "Bugle Notes," a book that cadets must memorize.

Promoted to the rank of colonel in 1838, Worth participated in the Second Seminole War in Florida. In 1842 Worth was instrumental in negotiating a settlement to that conflict, and this earned him promotion to brigadier general. Later, Worth's leadership at the Battle of Chapultepec in the Mexican-American War earned him a congressional sword of honor and promotion to major general.

Following the Mexican-American War, he commanded the Department of Texas, an Army department. He died of cholera in San Antonio in 1849. His remains were brought back to New York, where he was temporarily interred in Brooklyn's Green-Wood Cemetery. He was buried in his present location on November 25, 1857, following an elaborate procession of 6,500 soldiers.

FUN FACTS

1. The frontier post that he manned in Texas ultimately became the metropolis of Fort Worth.
2. In addition to the monument at Worth Square, Worth's native state also honored him with a street in downtown Manhattan: Worth Street.

Home of Franklin Delano Roosevelt
4097 ALBANY POST ROAD
HYDE PARK, NEW YORK 12538

In 1934 President Franklin Roosevelt had the National Archives created to better preserve our nation's history. In 1938 he decided that he wanted a presidential library to preserve his own presidential documents. The cornerstone was laid in 1939, and he formally dedicated the library on the grounds of his estate in Hyde Park, New York, on June

The Home of Franklin Delano Roosevelt at Hyde Park

30, 1941. In 2013 the library expanded its facilities to make Roosevelt's presidential records more easily accessible to historians and researchers. Today the FDR Presidential Library and Museum is administered appropriately by the National Archives.

The library is the centerpiece of the Hyde Park estate, a National Historic Site that also includes the president's house. The president and the First Lady are interred on the grounds, per FDR's wish, in the Rose Garden. Located in New York's Dutchess County, the Hyde Park estate is open nearly year-round to visitors and is administered by the National Park Service.

The museum hours are: November to March, 9 a.m. to 5 p.m.; April to October, 9 a.m. to 6 p.m. Tours of FDR's home are conducted by Park Rangers. There is an admission fee for entry to the grounds.

FRANKLIN DELANO ROOSEVELT
U.S. President
Born: January 30, 1882
Died: April 12, 1945

The FDR Presidential Library and Museum was the first presidential library we ever visited, and through the years we have been there a number of times. There is something awe-inspiring about not only the library, but also the house where FDR lived. It is hard to describe, but we both feel that, particularly within the house, FDR's spirit can still be felt. Just imagine yourself with the onus of creating policies to get the country through the Great Depression, which at its peak produced a 25% unemployment rate. In addition, consider the momentous strain FDR must have felt making life-and-death decisions during World War II. Finally, remember FDR's physical hardship: after losing the use of his legs to polio, he experienced daily pain for the rest of his life. If you ever want to feel history, as well as learn about it, please visit the Roosevelt estate.

FDR was born in Hyde Park, New York. He was a distant cousin to the nation's 26th president, Theodore Roosevelt. FDR graduated from Harvard in 1903 and later attended Columbia Law School. In 1905 he married his fifth cousin, Eleanor.

Like his famous cousin before him, Franklin served as assistant secretary of the Navy. In Franklin's case, this was during the administration of Woodrow Wilson. Roosevelt then ran for vice president in 1920 on the Democratic ticket with James Cox of Ohio. They were defeated (demolished is probably a better word) by Warren Harding and Calvin Coolidge. In 1921, while vacationing in Campobello Island, Roosevelt contracted polio. His paralysis was never formally divulged to the public by the press. Despite his physical disability, FDR was elected governor of New York in 1928. In 1932, at the height of the Great Depression, he ran against and easily defeated Herbert Hoover for the presidency.

Promising a New Deal for the American people, Roosevelt spoke directly to the public via radio programs, which became known as fireside chats. During these broadcasts, FDR explained his programs to address the economic situation by increasing the participation of the federal government in the economy. Congress quickly passed legislation to more closely regulate banks and create public sector jobs. By 1936 the economy, despite still being weak, had recovered sufficiently that FDR was reelected overwhelmingly.

Roosevelt won an unprecedented third term in 1940 with the threat of war in Europe looming. Following Japan's sneak attack on Pearl Harbor in December 1941, the US entered into World War II. With the aid of Great Britain's Winston Churchill and Russia's Joseph Stalin, FDR steered a clear and determined path that would eventually lead to the defeat of both Nazi Germany and the imperial forces of Japan.

In 1944 FDR was elected to a fourth term. However, he passed away less than three months following his fourth inauguration—just weeks before Hitler committed suicide, and several months before the surrender of Japan. Roosevelt succumbed to a stroke at his summer home at Warm Springs, Georgia, at the age of 63.

FUN FACTS

1. Though FDR was elected rather easily to the presidency four times, he never was able to carry the states of Maine and Vermont. Those states preferred Herbert Hoover in 1928, Alf Landon in 1936, Wendell Wilkie in 1940, and Tom Dewey in 1944.

2. If you haven't seen the 2012 movie *Hyde Park on Hudson*, please do so. Comedic actor Bill Murray, in a dramatic role, is excellent as FDR, and the movie offers a good perspective of the Roosevelt home.

ELEANOR ROOSEVELT
U.S. First Lady
Born: October 11, 1884
Died: November 7, 1962

Eleanor Roosevelt is the longest-serving First Lady in American history. She was also a diplomat, political and social activist, columnist, and radio show host. Though her marriage to Franklin was often troubled, Eleanor was always available to assist her husband with his political career and his health, particularly after he was diagnosed with polio.

Born in New York City, Anna Eleanor Roosevelt was the niece of President Theodore Roosevelt. Her childhood was often an unhappy

Franklin and Eleanor Roosevelt's Graves

one. She suffered from an inferiority complex as a child, and she lost both of her parents by the time she was 12. In 1905 she married her fifth cousin, Franklin. The marriage got off to a rocky start as Franklin's headstrong mother Sara, who had opposed the marriage, was constantly interfering. Throughout their marriage both Eleanor and Franklin allegedly had numerous affairs.

During Eleanor's tenure as First Lady she traveled thousands of miles, making public appearances to extol her husband's agenda to the American people. She wrote a regular weekly newspaper column, a monthly magazine column, and did a weekly radio show. She was particularly outspoken on the issues of women's rights and civil rights for African Americans. Eleanor Roosevelt was an advocate of government-operated daycare for the children of working women, and she fought for the integration of minorities into our armed services.

Following Franklin's death in 1945, Eleanor was an enthusiastic supporter of the United Nations and became its first U.S. delegate. She remained active in social and political affairs for the remainder of her life. Eleanor Roosevelt supported Adlai Stevenson in his two failed attempts at the presidency in the 1950s, and she supported, with reservations, John F. Kennedy for president in 1960. Eleanor's problem with JFK was his slowness in condemning Senator Joseph McCarthy's demagogic anticommunist tactics. She chaired the Kennedy administration's Presidential Commission on the Status of Women at the time of her death. She died at her apartment in New York City of cardiac failure in 1962. She was interred beside her husband in the Rose Garden at Hyde Park.

FUN FACTS

1. The Roosevelts' pet dog Fala, a black Scottish terrier, is arguably the most famous of all presidential pets. President Roosevelt took him everywhere on his travels. Fala was the centerpiece of a famous and humorous FDR speech criticizing Republicans for attacking not only him but also his "little dog Fala." Check out the speech on YouTube or another video outlet.

2. After Franklin passed away, Fala lived with Eleanor and they too became inseparable. Fala died in 1952 and is buried ten yards behind the Roosevelts' gravestone under a sundial.

Washington National Cathedral
3101 WISCONSIN AVENUE NW
WASHINGTON, DC 20016

This Episcopal cathedral was granted its charter by Congress in 1893. The construction of the Cathedral Church of St. Peter and St. Paul in the City and Diocese of Washington, better known as the Washington National Cathedral, was begun in 1907 and completed 83 years later in 1990. The cathedral's architecture is decidedly gothic, with pointed arches, flying buttresses, stained glass windows, and decorations of carved stone. Most of this structure was built using a buff-colored Indiana limestone.

Washington National Cathedral
(Courtesy of Washington National Cathedral)

The second largest cathedral in the United States (only St. John the Divine in New York City is larger), Washington National has been the site of funeral services for three U.S. presidents: Dwight Eisenhower, Ronald Reagan, and Gerald Ford. The hours are Monday through Friday, 10 a.m. to 5 p.m.; Saturday, 10 a.m. to 4 p.m. On Sunday worship services begin at 8 a.m., and sightseeing is allowed from 12:45 p.m. until 4 p.m.

WOODROW WILSON

U.S. President
Born: December 28, 1856
Died: February 3, 1924

As we discussed with respect to Ulysses Grant, we are fascinated when past presidential administrations are reassessed by historians and biographers. Though Grant's presidency appears to be on a slight upward trend, opinion on Woodrow Wilson's presidency seems to be headed in the opposite direction. This is because of allegations that Wilson held racist beliefs.

Woodrow Wilson's Tomb

Thomas Woodrow Wilson was born in Staunton, Virginia. The son of a Presbyterian minister, Wilson graduated from Princeton University in 1879 and then studied law at the University of Virginia. In 1883 Wilson entered Johns Hopkins University in Baltimore to study history and political science, and he received a Ph.D. in 1886. After serving as a professor at various institutions, such as Cornell University, Wilson was named the president of Princeton University in 1902 and held that post until 1910. Also in 1910, despite being a newcomer to New Jersey state politics, he secured the Democratic nomination for governor and was elected on a reform platform. Just two years later, in 1912, he won the Democratic nomination for president, and in November of that year defeated Republican incumbent William Howard Taft as well as Theodore Roosevelt, who ran as a third-party candidate.

As president Wilson pursued progressive legislation, including the Federal Reserve Act of 1913, the Federal Trade Commission Act of 1914, and the Clayton Antitrust Act of 1914. The first of these acts created a semiautonomous central bank that gave the government a more active role in the nation's currency. The second act put restrictions on unfair competition. The third act prohibited anticompetitive mergers.

Personal tragedy struck in 1914 when Wilson's first wife, Ellen Wilson, passed away from kidney failure. In 1915 Wilson met Edith Bolling Galt, and they were married at the end of the year.

When World War I broke out in Europe in 1914, the U.S. consensus opinion was to avoid involvement in foreign wars. In 1916 Woodrow Wilson ran for reelection on the slogan "He Kept Us Out of War," winning a close race over Republican Charles Evans Hughes. By April 1917, however, German attacks on American ships led Wilson to ask Congress to declare war.

The First World War concluded with an Allied victory in November 1918. Yet Wilson's dream of a League of Nations to help keep the peace was stymied when Republican senators rejected the Treaty of Versailles. On an extensive U.S. speaking tour on behalf of the treaty, Wilson suffered a major stroke on October 2, 1919, and he never fully recovered.

Incapacitated and aided greatly by his wife, Edith, Wilson was able to finish out his second term, which concluded in March 1921. Woodrow Wilson died in 1924 as the result of a second major stroke. Though

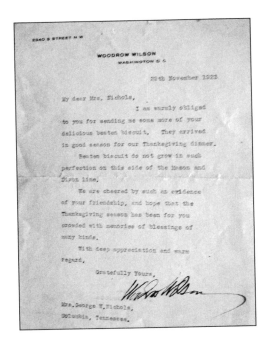

Letter Signed by Woodrow Wilson
(From the private collection of
Robert Gardino)

he was a devout Presbyterian, Edith was a devout Episcopalian, and it
was her decision to have her husband interred in an Episcopal church.

In the letter reproduced here, signed approximately nine weeks before his passing, one can see the effects of Wilson's stroke in his squig-
gly signature.

DIRECTIONS

The Wilson crypt, formally dedicated in 1956, can be found in a bay
immediately on the right when one enters the cathedral. Wilson's wife
Edith is entombed one level below, accessible via stairs.

EDITH WILSON

U.S. First Lady
Born: October 15, 1872
Died: December 28, 1961

Edith Bolling was born in Wytheville, Virginia, where she was home-
schooled by her paternal grandmother, Anne Bolling. Edith's grand-

mother encouraged her to appreciate music and poetry and to hold strong opinions.

In Washington, DC, circa 1895, Edith Bolling met Norman Galt, a prominent jeweler. They were married in 1896. In 1908 Galt died unexpectedly of a liver infection at the young age of 43. Edith's inheritance of her husband's estate and business funded many trips to Europe.

In March 1915 Edith was introduced to the recently widowed president of the United States, Woodrow Wilson. Love blossomed and they were married on December 18, 1915. Woodrow Wilson's debilitating stroke in October 1919 left him partially paralyzed and bedridden and affected his vision as well, but he was completely insulated by his wife and his physician, Dr. Cary Grayson. Not even Vice President Thomas Riley Marshall was permitted to see him. Edith Wilson herself determined what matters of state were important to bring to the attention of the disabled president. Edith, in essence, assumed many of the duties of the executive branch of government. President Wilson

Edith Wilson's Crypt

eventually recovered partially, going from a wheelchair to a cane, and was then able to attend cabinet meetings.

After President Wilson passed away in 1924, Edith remained active, serving as director of the Woodrow Wilson National Fellowship Foundation and head of the Woman's National Democratic Club. The goal of the Wilson Foundation is the identification and development of leaders. Edith Wilson died as the result of congestive heart failure in 1961 at the age of 89. She bequeathed her house to the National Trust for Historic Preservation, which opened it as a museum in 1964.

HELEN KELLER
Author/Lecturer
Born: June 27, 1880
Died: June 1, 1968

We were first drawn to Helen Keller when, sometime in the mid-1960s, our grammar school did a rare thing by showing a movie to all grades in the school auditorium. It was *The Miracle Worker*, released in 1962, starring Patty Duke as the young Helen Keller and Anne Bancroft as Keller's teacher, Anne Sullivan. Needless to say, Keller's early struggles made an impression on us.

Helen Keller was born in Tuscumbia, Alabama. At the age of 19 months she fell sick, probably with either scarlet fever or meningitis, and as a result she became deaf and blind. In 1886 her parents conferred with Alexander Graham Bell, who was working with deaf children at the time. Bell directed them to the Perkins Institute for the Blind, then located in Boston, and it was there that they met Anne Sullivan. Sullivan, herself visually impaired, soon became Helen's instructor. This began a relationship that would last a remarkable 49 years. Sullivan's teaching method consisted of spelling words into Helen's palm while Helen's other hand touched the corresponding object. Sullivan's job was not easy, as Helen would throw tantrums and at first resisted learning anything new from this new person in her life. The breakthrough in communication between the two came with the word "water," with cool water running over one of Keller's hands.

Keller's formal education began in 1888 with her attendance at the Perkins Institute, followed in 1894 by work at the Horace Mann

Crypt of Helen Keller, Anne Sullivan, and Polly Thomson

School for the Deaf in New York City. She and Sullivan then returned to Massachusetts, where Helen attended the Cambridge School for Young Ladies before gaining admittance to Radcliffe College. In 1904, at age 24, Keller became the first deaf and blind person to earn a bachelor of arts degree. Keller wanted to learn how to speak and did so by learning to "hear" people's speech by reading their lips with her hands.

Keller soon began giving speeches and lectures, which she did for the rest of her life. In addition to advocacy for people with disabilities, she was a suffragette, pacifist, radical socialist, and birth control advocate. She also wrote 12 books, the most noteworthy being her autobiography, *The Story of My Life* in 1903.

Anne Sullivan passed away in 1936 after a heart attack. Because of her work in teaching the disabled, Sullivan was the first woman honored by interment in the Washington National Cathedral. Following Sullivan's death, Keller's secretary Mary Agnes "Polly" Thomson became Keller's companion until Thomson's death in 1960. In 1964

Keller was awarded the Presidential Medal of Freedom by President Lyndon B. Johnson. Helen Keller succumbed to the effects of a series of strokes and died in 1968. It was fitting that Keller's remains were interred next to those of her dear friend and teacher Anne Sullivan in the Washington National Cathedral.

FUN FACTS

1. In 1916, at the age of 36, Keller had a love affair with Peter Fagan, a young *Boston Herald* reporter who was sent to her home to function as Keller's secretary when Anne Sullivan took ill. They became secretly engaged, and she defied her family by attempting to elope with Fagan. When Keller's mother found out about the plans, she intervened and the marriage never took place.
2. Both of Helen's eyes were replaced with glass replicas for medical and cosmetic reasons.

GEORGE DEWEY
Navy Admiral
Born: December 26, 1837
Died: January 16, 1917

When we were kids, we loved throwing around memorable quotes to produce a laugh. Looking back, we can thank a number of American naval commanders for quotes we used in our smart-aleck days. Admiral George Dewey gave us a quote that we used at the start of snowball fights: "Fire when ready, Gridley." When we discovered that Admiral Dewey's remains were in the Washington National Cathedral, we thought it fitting to include him in this book.

George Dewey was born in Montpelier, Vermont. After graduating from the U.S. Naval Academy in 1858, Midshipman Dewey was given assignments on battleships that patrolled the Mediterranean. At the outbreak of the Civil War, Dewey was made an executive lieutenant and assigned to the *USS Mississippi* under Admiral David Farragut. Dewey distinguished himself by demonstrating excellent navigation skills under threat of battle. Farragut had Dewey appointed executive officer on the *USS Colorado*, and in 1864 Dewey distinguished himself

George Dewey's Tomb

again in the Battles of Fort Fisher. Dewey was soon promoted to lieutenant commander.

Following the Civil War, Dewey remained in the Navy. He toured Europe as well as the Asian Pacific regions. In 1893 Dewey was transferred to Washington, DC, and in 1896, with the rank of commodore, he was placed on the Board of Inspection and Survey. In 1897, sensing war with Spain was imminent and feeling restless at the inaction of Washington, he applied for sea duty in the Philippines.

It was in the Spanish-American War that Dewey gained everlasting fame. On board the *USS Olympia*, George Dewey commanded a fleet of seven battleships. In Manila Bay on May 1, 1898, he uttered his immortal words, "You may fire when you are ready, Gridley," to Captain Charles Gridley. In just six hours, his battleships sank or captured the entire Spanish fleet. He was quickly promoted to rear admiral. The following year, Dewey was promoted to full admiral. Upon his return to the United States, Dewey was given a hero's welcome, with victory parades in his honor in New York, Boston, and Washington, DC.

In 1900 he was named president of the newly established General Board of the Navy Department, which functioned as the Navy's major policy-making body. He served on the board until his death in 1917. From 1903 on, he enjoyed the special rank of admiral of the navy.

FUN FACT

Dewey remains the only American awarded the title of admiral of the navy.

Thomas Edison National Historical Park

211 MAIN STREET
WEST ORANGE, NEW JERSEY 07052

The National Park Service administers the Thomas Edison National Historical Park, which contains the laboratory where Edison worked until his death in 1931. The museum collection is ranked as the third largest in the National Park Service. Examples of what can be found in the museum are early electric bulbs, phonograph records, and an electric generator used by Edison in his lab. Edison's home Glenmont,

The Home of Thomas Edison

which he purchased for his bride Mina in 1886, is also part of the park. Edison and Mina are buried together behind the house.

Tours are provided by Park Rangers. Tickets are sold on a first-come, first-served basis. From fall through spring, the laboratory is open Wednesday through Sunday, 10 a.m. to 4 p.m. In summer it is open Wednesday through Sunday, 10:00 a.m. to 5 p.m. The residence, Glenmont House, is open only on Saturday and Sunday.

THOMAS ALVA EDISON
Inventor
Born: February 11, 1847
Died: October 18, 1931

For one of us, Thomas Edison's autograph was an early important autograph purchase. Bought at an auction approximately 25 years ago, it usually produces a "Wow" reaction when we show our collection to friends or guests. This piece is a commemorative envelope with postage stamps commemorating Edison's invention of the electric light bulb. He signed it approximately two years before his death.

Commemorative Envelope Signed by Thomas Edison
(From the private collection of Robert Gardino)

Known as the "Wizard of Menlo Park," Thomas Edison ranks as arguably the most prolific inventor of all time, having held a total of 1,093 patents! Edison was born in Milan, Ohio, but grew up mostly in Port Huron, Michigan. He attended school for only a short time and was taught mostly at home by his mother. Early in his childhood he became hard of hearing, probably as the result of scarlet fever.

Edison started his working life as a telegraph operator in Port Huron. Later, when he worked for Western Union in Louisville, Kentucky, his love of tinkering and experiment caused him to be fired when he accidentally spilled sulfuric acid on his boss's desk.

Edison married his first wife, Mary, in 1871, and they had three children together. She died in 1884 of a brain tumor. In 1886 the 39-year-old Edison married Mina Miller, who was only 20 at the time. They also had three children together.

His first patent was for an electric vote recorder in 1869. Edison's first industrial research lab was built in 1876 in Menlo Park, New Jersey. After he moved to Glenmont in 1887, he established a lab here and another in Fort Myers, Florida. It was in these labs that Edison created his impressive list of inventions that improved the American way of life, including the light bulb, phonograph, movie camera, fluoroscope, stock ticker, improved telephone receiver, storage battery, and an improved process for rubber manufacturing.

Edison kept company with industrial giants Henry Ford and Harvey Firestone. Together they enjoyed camping outdoors. However, Edison did not take long vacations. He was a tireless worker and active to the end. Edison inaugurated the Lackawanna Railroad in September 1930 by driving the train for one mile as it left the Hoboken depot.

Thomas Edison died from complications of diabetes in 1931 at his New Jersey home, Glenmont.

FUN FACTS

1. Edison's last breath is preserved in a test tube at the Henry Ford Museum near Detroit. Henry Ford reportedly requested that Edison's son Charles capture his father's dying breath and send the tube as a memento to Ford's museum.
2. Edison's favorite invention was the phonograph. He referred to it as "my baby." Edison worked on this invention longer than on any other invention, making improvements over 52 years.

MINA MILLER EDISON
Activist
Born: July 6, 1865
Died: August 24, 1947

Mina Miller was born in Ohio to a well-to-do and respected family. Her father, Lewis, was an inventor as well as a manufacturer. Lewis's inventions mostly involved agricultural equipment.

Mina Miller was only 20 when she married the 39-year-old Thomas Edison in 1885; it was his second marriage. Thomas Edison would later recount that, when he and Mina were courting, he taught her Morse code so they could converse privately when family was around. In fact, Thomas Edison claimed he proposed to Mina in Morse code, and she responded with a "yes."

A civic-minded person, Mina was instrumental in establishing the West Orange Community League, which offered recreational and cultural programs, such as summer camp for the young and forums

Thomas and Mina Edison's Graves

for invited speakers to discuss topics of interest. Mina was also very involved with the Chautauqua Institution, a not-for-profit religious and cultural education center for youths and adults. Mina's family maintained a summer home in Chautauqua, New York, and Mina's father cofounded the institution. In 1947 Mina Edison donated her winter home as a botanical garden to Fort Myers, Florida, as a memorial to her husband. Shortly after her donation, she died as the result of heart failure.

FUN FACT

One of Thomas and Mina's sons, Theodore, also became an inventor. One of Theodore's inventions was a stereoscopic mapping instrument that created the illusion of depth in an image.

Christ Church Burial Ground
5TH AND ARCH STREETS
PHILADELPHIA, PENNSYLVANIA 19106

Christ Church, at 20 N. American Street, is an Episcopal church founded in 1695. The church graveyard, a few blocks away, is unique in that not only Ben Franklin, but also four other signers of the Declaration of Independence are buried there.

The burial ground was originally enclosed behind brick walls, but sometime in the 1850s Franklin's descendants requested that the wall

Christ Church
Burial Ground

in front of his grave contain an opening so that people could see it from the street. Subsequently a metal fence was put up, and now people on the street can see not only Franklin's grave but most of the other graves. Many take the liberty, as a tribute, of tossing a penny on Franklin's slab (a penny saved is a penny earned).

The Burial Ground is open from March through November. The hours are Monday to Saturday, 10 a.m. to 4 p.m., and Sunday, 12 p.m. to 4 p.m. There is a small fee for entering. Tours are also available.

BENJAMIN FRANKLIN
Founding Father/Inventor/Diplomat
Born: January 17, 1706
Died: April 17, 1790

When we first visited Philadelphia, we took in the historical sights such as Independence Hall, the Liberty Bell, the home of Betsy Ross, the Franklin Institute science museum, and the South 9th Street Italian Market. And as respectable (we hope) grave trippers, how could we bypass the grave of one of America's most famous citizens?

Benjamin Franklin was arguably America's first rock star. He was a statesman, author, printer, scientist, inventor, postmaster, civic activist, governor, and one of our most accomplished diplomats. A man for all seasons and then some!

Franklin learned about the printing business at a very young age as an apprentice in his brother's printing shop in Boston. In 1723 he left his brother's shop and took up residence in Philadelphia, where he set up his own print shop. In a few years' time, he became the publisher of the *Pennsylvania Gazette*, a newspaper that earned him a reputation for skillful commentary on the issues of the day. In 1733 he published *Poor Richard's Almanac*, which was an instant success and became a part of American culture. The almanac, like most other almanacs, contained a calendar, weather information, poetry, as well as astronomical and astrological data. However, its popularity came mostly from Franklin's maxims, such as "Well done is better than well said" and "Haste makes waste."

Franklin's keen mind led him to a number of scientific discoveries and inventions. Some of his inventions include the Franklin stove,

Benjamin Franklin's Grave

bifocal glasses, and the lightning rod. In his most famous experiment, in 1752, he flew a kite with a key attached in a storm, proving that lightning and electricity were the same.

Over the course of approximately 20 years, ending in the mid-1770s, Franklin spent considerable time in London for various political missions, as well as for scientific research and experiment. After his final stay in London, Franklin returned to America and devoted much of his energy to colonial independence.

In 1776, along with John Adams and Thomas Jefferson, he edited the original draft of the Declaration of Independence. During the Revolutionary War, as ambassador to France, he secured favorable treatment and aid from France for the colonies. Franklin was also a delegate to the Constitutional Convention in 1787. In his later years, he wrote many essays that stressed the importance of abolishing slavery in the new nation.

In the final stages of his life, Franklin suffered from multiple ailments, most notably painful episodes of the gout. Benjamin Franklin died in 1790 as the result of complications from pleurisy (a disease of the lungs). The nation went into mourning. His funeral drew approximately 20,000 citizens who wished to convey their respects to their revered giant.

FUN FACT

The *Bonhomme Richard*, the ship that Revolutionary War hero John Paul Jones commanded in his victorious sea battle with the British ship the *Serapis*, was named as a tribute to Ben Franklin. Bonhomme Richard was an indirect reference to Franklin's *Poor Richard's Almanac*.

Graceland
ELVIS PRESLEY BOULEVARD
MEMPHIS, TENNESSEE 38116

Graceland, home of rock superstar Elvis Presley during the last 20 years of his life, was designated a National Historic Landmark in 2006. Graceland averages more than 600,000 visitors a year, more than any other American tourist site except the White House. The name Graceland was given to the property by prior owners, but Elvis liked

Graceland

the name and kept it when he purchased the estate in 1957. Graceland was opened to the public in 1982.

The 13.8-acre estate contains not only the Presley mansion, but also other complexes that exhibit his gold and platinum singles and albums, movie memorabilia, concert jumpsuits, autos, motorcycles, and Elvis's two private jets, the *Lisa Marie* and *Hound Dog II*. The Meditation Garden of the estate contains the graves of Elvis, his mother and father, and his fraternal grandmother.

Tickets must be purchased to gain access. The estate is usually open every day except Thanksgiving and Christmas, with the most common hours being Monday through Saturday, 8:30 a.m. to 5 p.m., and Sunday, 9:30 a.m. to 4 p.m.

ELVIS PRESLEY
Entertainer
Born: January 8, 1935
Died: August 16, 1977

One of us is a huge Elvis Presley fan, owning a certified gold album as well as a certified platinum single. We have visited Graceland twice, and if we should be so fortunate to get Grave Trippers on television, we would love to do a segment on "The King" from Graceland.

Elvis was born in Tupelo, Mississippi, in 1935. When he was 13, he and his parents moved to Memphis. Elvis was at best an average student, but he loved music and wanted to sing. After high school Elvis studied to become an electrician, but one day he went to Sun Records' studio to make, for a small fee, a recording of his own. Sam Phillips, the owner of Sun Records, was impressed by Presley's voice and invited him back to record some more songs with backup from two respected musicians.

In 1954 history was made with Elvis's first commercial single, "That's All Right." It was an instant regional hit in the South. Elvis began touring the South's small clubs and fairs. His gyrations on stage caused a sensation, and in less than two years Sun Records sold Elvis's contract to larger recording label RCA Victor. Soon after, Elvis hired Colonel Tom Parker as his manager. Parker was an experienced manager of show business talent, such as country legend Hank Snow.

Elvis Presley's Grave (Courtesy of Shutterstock)

Parker knew a good thing when he saw one, and he quickly got Elvis national exposure with TV appearances on *The Ed Sullivan Show*, *The Steve Allen Show*, and *The Milton Berle Show*. This publicity led to a movie contract with producer Hal Wallis. Elvis's first feature film was 1956's *Love Me Tender*. Also in 1956, Elvis recorded his first gold single, "Heartbreak Hotel." That monster hit was quickly followed in the same year with "I Want You, I Need You, I Love You," "Don't Be Cruel," and the explosive "Hound Dog." All of these were also gold singles.

In 1958 Elvis was drafted into the Army and served for two years. His two-year public absence did not affect his enormous popularity. His 1960 recordings of "Stuck On You," "It's Now or Never," and "Are You Lonesome Tonight?" were enormous international hits.

In 1961 Elvis stopped doing live shows, and he averaged three feature films a year through the 1960s. By 1967 it was obvious that Elvis's often silly-scripted movies and soundtracks were no longer popular with the public. Rock 'n' roll competitors like the Beatles, the Rolling Stones, the Who, Led Zeppelin, and the Mamas and the Papas were dominating the music charts. Elvis was in danger of becoming irrelevant in the music world.

The King was reborn, however, with a television special that aired on December 3, 1968. Many argue (and we concur) that Elvis never sounded or looked better than he did on that Singer Sewing Machine–sponsored special. The demand for him to return to live performances was overwhelming, and in 1969 he opened to critical acclaim at the International Hotel in Las Vegas. In 1973 his career peaked with his worldwide satellite show *Elvis: Aloha from Hawaii.* It has been estimated that, counting rebroadcasts, more than a billion people may have watched that special.

However, the years 1972–1973 saw the beginning of Elvis's physical deterioration from excess touring and his weight gain that stemmed from poor diet and prescription drug abuse. Also, his wife, Priscilla, devastated Elvis by divorcing him. To the very end, despite his bloated appearance, Elvis remained popular with his legion of fans, performing to sold-out concerts wherever he appeared. Elvis Presley died on August 16, 1977, most likely because the simultaneous use of multiple drugs led to heart failure.

FUN FACTS

1. Despite the enormous number of gold hits Elvis produced in his life, he won only three Grammy awards. All were for gospel recordings.

2. To achieve a proper mood for the recording of "Are You Lonesome Tonight?" Elvis requested that the lights be turned off in the recording studio. If you listen closely to the very end of the song (best to use headphones), you will hear a sort of click. That was Elvis accidentally knocking over a chair.

Acknowledgments

The authors wish to acknowledge the following for their assistance and hard work in helping us put together this *Grave Trippers* volume. Several people provided photographs; they are mentioned below and cited in the photo captions. All photos not otherwise credited were taken by the authors.

To our publisher, Edward Jutkowitz, we wish to express our deepest thanks for his belief and enthusiasm for our project, and for bringing our book to fruition.

To our editor, Douglas Gordon, for his hard work and for his expertise in the art of cogent writing that brought our volume to a higher level.

We extend our unending gratitude to Vince and Denise De Giaimo for their yeoman efforts and expense in gathering essential data used in this book.

For providing us with exquisite photos, we thank Joe Connor.

And to many others we extend our deep gratitude:

To Robert and Patrice Martin, for their love, encouragement, and guidance for all these years. Bob, you are a great patriot!!! Patrice, you are simply the best!!!

To Ken and Kris Donovan, whose connections eventually led to the making of this book. (If you don't like the book, blame them.)

To Helene Stapinski, whose advice and guidance helped us smooth out our beginners' rough edges.

A special acknowledgment to John and Melissa Capuano, who not only supplied some of our photographs, but whose macabre minds conceived of the creation of *Grave Trippers*.

To Vivian Lee of NY1 News, for fighting for us to appear on her
weekend program *Spotlight* and being a Grave Tripper supporter from the beginning.

To Jeanne Straus, President and CEO of Straus Media, who has
always been there for us with ideas, encouragement, and
support.

To Dominic Bruzzese, who cheerfully helped us navigate some
of those dangerous and curvy cemetery roads, among other
things.

To Joel Olicker, Co-Founder and CEO, and Robert Kirwan,
Executive Producer, of Powderhouse Productions. Joel, thank
you for suggesting the name of *Grave Trippers*, and Robert, for
producing our exquisitely done videos. You guys can make
anyone look good.

To Susan and Don Lukenbill, for their services in the making of
this book.

To David Gilliam of Hollywood Cemetery, who quickly provided
photos of key sites at the cemetery when we were in need.

To Barbara Selesky of Woodlawn Cemetery, who provided us
with detailed directions and made our navigation much
simpler.

To David Gurmai of Laurel Hill Cemetery, who graciously guided
us through the twists and turns of that scenic cemetery.

To Torrence Thomas and Scott Sanders, who provided access to
some hard-to-find crypts in the Washington National Cathedral. Thanks also to Kevin Eckstrom for providing a great
photo of this national landmark.

To Frank Sorace, whose friendship we truly value, after all these
years, and are grateful to have.

To Dr. Stanley Fahn and his wife Charlotte, for their friendship
and for keeping us healthy.

To Patrick Hogan, yoga instructor extraordinaire.

To Deepali Lewis, who as our physical therapist has whipped us
into shape, and to her husband David for his friendship and
kindness.

To Franco and Marina Ferrari, for always checking up on us.

To Glenn Askin, a true friend, who is always ready to lend us a helping hand whenever she can.

To SunHi and Gary Schwartz, who have taken care of our minds and bodies and given enthusiastic support to *Grave Trippers*.

To Adrienne and Paul Connolly, who always have smiles on their faces (why, we don't know) and have been with us in good times and bad.

To Linda Meilan, who is a sister to us, has been a part of our family for nearly 40 years, and has seen us through thick and thin.

To Bill and Patty Siegel, who, if asked how long they have known the Gardino brothers, might say "Too long!" We love them anyway.

To David and Marla Feinberg, who never stopped encouraging us and whose friendship we value.

To Charles and Joan Salomon, who always treat us with grace and a touch of class, for providing us with insider information for this book.

To Al Cattabiani, who since the inception of this project has provided us with his best efforts on our behalf.

To our cousins Nino and Marilena Soave, who always see to our needs and make sure we are well despite the distance between us.

To Marisa Gaffoglio, who is our eyes and ears in Italy and has been a steadfast friend of our family.

Finally, to Larry David, whose comedic genius inspired the title of this book. Thanks for all the laughs!